To Keir
Always Write
Love

Jane
Savy

CW00520086

HERE THEY COME WITH THEIR MAKE-UP ON

suede, *coming up* ... and more
adventures beyond the wild frontiers

JANE SAVIDGE

For Mum, Dad, Michèle,
Kle, Scout, and Piper.

HERE THEY COME WITH THEIR MAKE-UP ON
Suede, *Coming Up* ... And More
Adventures Beyond The Wild Frontiers
Jane Savidge

A Jawbone book
First edition 2022
Published in the UK and the USA by
Jawbone Press
Office G1
141–157 Acre Lane
London SW2 5UA
England
www.jawbonepress.com

ISBN 978-1-911036-89-0

Printed by Short Run Press, Exeter, Devon

1 2 3 4 5 26 25 24 23 22

contents

COMING UP: A TIMELINE

years before the present:

4.5 billion approx.—formation of the planet earth.

2.5 billion approx.—evolution of the genus *homo* in africa.

300,000 approx.—daily usage of fire.

200 approx.—the industrial revolution.

25 approx.—release of the third suede album, *coming up*.

Suede

From Wikipedia, the free encyclopaedia

Suede (pronounced /sweɪd/(*SWAYD*)) is a type of leather with a napped finish, commonly used for jackets, shoes, shirts, purses, furniture, and other items. The term comes from the French *gants de Suède*, which literally means 'gloves from Sweden'.

Suede is made from the underside of the animal skin, which is softer and more pliable than, though not as durable as, the outer skin layer.

PRELUDE

Suede's third album, *Coming Up*, is a record that was perhaps not meant to be. The band had arrived fully formed at the start of 1992, just as a *Melody Maker* front cover proclaimed them 'the best new band in Britain'. They were yet to release a single and would spend the next twelve months gracing the front covers of eighteen magazines in the UK before their debut album was released.

That eponymous debut long-player became the most eagerly awaited record since *Never Mind The Bollocks* by the Sex Pistols and went straight to no.1. The album turned out to be the biggest-selling debut since Frankie Goes To Hollywood's *Welcome To The Pleasure Dome*, but just over a year after that, on the eve of the release of their second album, *Dog Man Star*, and in the most dramatic of circumstances, half the band's songwriting partnership—in the shape of lead guitarist Bernard Butler—upped sticks and left. Lead singer Brett Anderson now headed up a three-piece forced to behave as if nothing had happened.

Brett immediately recruited a seventeen-year-old schoolboy/guitarist who found himself—together with the rest of the band—promoting a record Suede no longer loved or cared for. Naturally, whilst all this internal drama was playing itself out, the media came to their own conclusions: the band were incapable of recording a decent song ever again. To make matters worse, whilst Suede had noticeably retreated to the sidelines, bands like Pulp, Blur, and Oasis now dominated the musical landscape.

Enter *Coming Up*.

Coming Up was supposed to sound the death knell of Suede, the band that kickstarted Britpop. Instead, it resulted in Brett entering an early midlife crisis, an all-consuming drug addiction, and an arena of media and public scrutiny usually reserved for disgraced politicians.

This is the story of how Brett and Suede emerged from the chaotic ruined remnants of their career and set about stumping their most ardent critics by writing and recording an album that turned out to be their most widely appreciated and commercially successful album to date.

It is also a personal excursion into the heart of an album that I love—if not unconditionally then as a piece of work that has ultimately survived the ravages of time—as well as the brutish nasty, and not-so-short nature of the media scrutiny that had threatened to confine Suede to the dustbin of history.[*] It's a story involving the sheer bloody-mindedness of it all, and a journey of self-realisation that no one has truly appreciated.

Until now.

---

[*] Warning: may contain traces of me.

1

TAXI FOR EVERYONE

❝I once considered placing an ad in the *Time Out* Lonely Hearts section. *Vegan golfer seeks spinster librarian for fun and games*, it was supposed to read, until I realised I had to pay by the letter. But which letters or words should I get rid of? The *fun and games?*❞

'We are addressing the real issues of sexuality. We're talking about the used condom as opposed to the beautiful bed.'

Way back in 1992, when I used to be someone—hey, it's called *living the dream*—Savage & Best, the PR company I'd recently set up with John Best, found ourselves looking after UK indie-rock superstars Curve, Jesus & Mary Chain, and Spiritualized on their *Rollercoaster* tour of the USA. The tour also boasted US noiseniks Medicine—who we also looked after—although they didn't feature on the bill terribly often, perhaps due to the fact that there may have been some serious drug issues involved. The tour kicked off on October 23 and was in full swing by the time I arrived in San Francisco on November 19.

Curve's lead partners in crime, Toni Halliday and Dean Garcia, had been kind enough to send a limo to pick me up at the airport, and when I'd finally argued my way past Immigration Control, I noticed a driver clutching a sign saying *Ms Savidge* and was led to a car that could have only been reserved for an indie princess such as myself. Naturally, I am being disingenuous, although I did think at the time, *Is this how I am going to travel from now on?* You'll be relieved to know it wasn't—you are not such a gentle reader after all—but the trip proved hugely memorable, nonetheless.

San Francisco felt like some kind of spiritual home—I thought the same of Amsterdam at the time—and I loved the bookshops and the people in that order. I think I may have been particularly confused by the community of bearded crossdressers that I stumbled across whilst looking for any girls who looked as intriguing as I did. Of course, I was—and still am—so crap at finding anyone remotely connected to the nature of what I am looking for that I once considered placing an ad in the *Time Out* 'Lonely Hearts' section. 'Vegan golfer seeks spinster librarian for fun and games,' it was supposed to read, until I realised I had to pay by the letter. But which letters or words should I get rid of? The *fun and games*? I couldn't decide, so the advert never materialised, and I wasn't to meet the spinster or librarian—anyone knows, you can't have both—who would break my heart. As you will have guessed, this was many years before the internet reinforced my opinion that a search for a suitable partner could still prove fruitless: even when promoting oneself to a worldwide audience of spinsters and librarians who shared my emotional preferences, the cupboard remained bare.

At the hotel, Toni and Dean greeted me like we were old friends—which in fact we were—and we shared champagne and other frivolities, before an arranged dinner featuring extended members of the Curve entourage intervened. Of course, I included myself in this extended entourage, but I've often wondered how these symbiotic relationships work themselves out: I am clever enough to realise that, if charged with enhancing the public profile of an artist, then I am a useful person for that artist to become friends with, but I am also vain enough to believe that I am interesting enough (!) to bypass the usual ground rules surrounding one's place in the artist's immediate field of vision; the combination of these two seemingly contradictory standpoints has ensured that I have never outstayed my welcome, nor indeed ignored the welcome mat of possibility that's always laid on. Naturally, this is my way of saying that I don't know where I belong, and that you should never marry a pop star. But you can have fun trying, nonetheless.

The welcome mat of possibility? I've got you there, haven't I?

Toni and Dean always seemed older than I was—even though only one of them fitted this description—a conclusion I must have come to because I associated the pair's constant travels around the globe with their worldly-wise appeal. Now that we had met overseas for the first time, there appeared to be an unspoken agreement that we had entered a new phase of our relationship.

The dinner proved uneventful, but the next day's show was one of the best I'd ever seen, even if it was marred by an in-house spat involving the Brothers Grimm that were the Mary Chain. I witnessed the semi-violent, semi-serious sibling skirmish in the dressing room; the squabbling eventually transferred itself onto the stage, where it became apparent that Jim and William would not be on speaking terms for the rest of the tour. Either that or they would be sharing a cup of tea and a scone before they went to bed.

Having said that, the Mary Chain's performance was all the better for the inner turmoil engendered by the duo's evidently long-held grudges, and the attendant displays by Spiritualized and

Curve of outlandish techno brilliance meant that the audience never knew what hit them.

After the show, each band, together with their entourages, piled into their giant tour buses—intended to ensure a good night's sleep—whilst we all made our way overnight to Los Angeles for the next evening's show. Naturally, no sleep was involved—I can only vouch for my own miserable attempts in this regard—and our arrival in LA coincided with a hangover of epic dimensions, compounded by the news that the day rooms we had arranged to crash in were nowhere near ready. Everyone disappeared off with their allotted chums for the day, and I went shopping.

We were staying at the Mondrian, which was—and probably still is—my hotel of choice, although on a subsequent trip to LA I found myself staying at the Chateau Marmont, and the whole episode proved to be something of a drama.[*] On this occasion,

---

[*] The Chateau had a reputation for fast living, since John Belushi—of *Blues Brothers* notoriety—had ended his life there after a suitable period of self-abuse. I can assure you that Belushi's demise, and the hotel's notoriety as a party hotspot, played no part in my decision to stay there, since I have always hated the *Blues Brothers* movie as it bore no relation to my version of music's Year Zero, but I was booked in there by a client and that was that.

Once I was ensconced within the confines of the Chateau, I took solace in the fact that I was privileged enough to have been awarded a cabin in the grounds. However, I soon realised that I had been unfortunate enough to be allocated a cabin without functioning air conditioning. I am the kind of woman who prefers the Arctic to the Amazon and thinks you should put on a knitted jumpsuit rather than a thermostat, so the prospect of staying in the room for longer than the few minutes it would take to put on some make up and get ready to go out, was not something I could contemplate.

however, with Curve in tow, I was happy to be in a space I understood, and where the hotel staff were one day going to understand me.

This was the first overseas trip where I discovered the delights of a hotel corner suite—some of you may have noticed on previous occasions how very grounded I am about such things. After I returned from my shopping trip, I dumped my bags in my 'quarters' and got ready for the evening ahead. Two hours later, I took a cab to the venue, arriving far too early for someone of my stature but at least early enough to watch each band in turn tout their astonishing wares live on stage. I soon began to realise that the collection of UK acts I had accompanied on my overseas

---

I rang the front desk and asked if they could fix the air conditioning. They couldn't, but they did agree to send someone to my room with a portable air conditioning unit. However, once the contraption was installed, the device proved to be so unbearably loud and cumbersome that there was no way the pair of us could have spent any length of time of together. One of us had to go.

I rang the front desk again, politely asking if the unit could be taken back to where it came from. And then I ordered some olives.

'I am sorry, madam,' said the voice of doom from the depths of hell, 'but we have run out of olives.'

This was the last straw—or it would have been if I'd attempted to order straws on room service and they only had one left—so I packed my bags and made my way to reception. Once there, I tracked down the first member of staff unlucky enough to slide into view, making a point of sighing like a spoilt supermodel, who'd just been told her usual hairdresser was on holiday. As politely as possible, I informed her that I no longer had need of the hotel's services.

'Would you be kind enough to book me a room at the Mondrian?' I enquired.

The woman was kind enough to do so, and also kind enough to book me a cab to take me the fifty yards across the road to where the Mondrian was situated.

travels were of an entirely different order to anything, young American audiences were yet used to.

Naturally, I am overemphasising a point to make a point, but I still feel the need to indulge you, nonetheless: I am aware that bands like the Ramones, the Stooges, the Velvets, the New York Dolls—haven't we been here before?—possess rock'n'roll gumption in abundance, but their real significance lies in the fact that they are a diversionary means of distracting us from the actual *State Of The Union*. To wit, and for reasons I cannot fathom, I had come to the conclusion that British bands existed for their own amusement and American bands existed for the entertainment of others. If you've ever tried to explain the merits of the Manic Street Preachers—back in their 90s heyday—to as many of your American friends as would listen, you will know what I mean:

The band feature a drop-dead gorgeous guitarist who often appears on stage without his guitar plugged-in, you might say, *and he writes a significant amount of the lyrics for the singer who may not actually have a direct grasp of what he is singing about. Oh, and their bass player wears a dress and sometimes says things like, 'let's hope they build a motorway over this fucking shithole'*—whilst performing at Glastonbury—*or 'here's hoping Michael Stipe goes the same way as Freddie Mercury'*—at Kilburn National Ballroom—*just because he's angry.*

If I've lost my American readers for a moment, then I apologise, but if there's a chance of persuading any of them back, here goes: when Britpop darlings Suede made their inaugural trip to the

14

USA in 1994, Brett found himself on the David Letterman show, tasked with the opportunity of promoting the band's forthcoming US tour.

'What kind of music do you listen to?' asked Letterman of our celebrated, decorous English pop star.

Brett was sitting uncomfortably on a chair, surely provided as a conduit for persuading the American heartland to fall in love with all matters Suede.

Oh, I listen to Aerosmith, and Journey and Boston, was the expected response, as a way to connect with the show's regular audience.

'Oh, I just listen to Suede,' said Brett, with the casual insouciance we have come to associate with our intrepid hero.

And there, in a puff of smoke, went the band's chances of cracking America.

And that's why I love them.

* * *

After the show, I made my way to Curve's dressing room, as I couldn't see how I was expected to blend in amongst the likes of Spiritualized or the Scary Chain; Savage & Best may have been charged with representing both bands, but I was already identifiably associated with Suede, and Spiritualized were John and Melissa's baby, and the Scary Chain were not directly represented by me either. And, as Jim Reid was dating Polly from S&B at the time, I must have been seen as a necessary yet divisive presence on the tour, and one that didn't need to be encouraged.*

In the dressing room, Curve mainstays Toni, Dean, Monti, and Alex were in that state of euphoria-tinged-with-despair that often

---

* If some of my readers are wondering why I rarely write about my experiences accompanying Suede to ever more far-flung destinations around the globe, then, well, that's because I never felt the need to tempt any British music magazine or newspaper with such frivolities. Indeed, unlike most artists of the 90s—or any other era for that matter—Suede were so instantly press-worthy that it was all I could do to slow everyone the fuck down. Admittedly, I remember being an ever-present phenomenon on several Suede press trips to exotic locations such as Denmark, Iceland, and Hong Kong, but these were the exception rather than the rule. Suffice to say that when gaining press coverage for one of your clients proves tricky, it's many the PR that's plucked Australia out of her handbook, waving the prospect of a trip Down Under to any newspaper editor willing to Air Mile themselves up—and all for the promise of a front cover or any other coverage deemed appropriate to the jaunt. I've often wondered whether the general public were aware that it was common practice for record companies and music publicists in the 90s to pay thousands of pounds on planes and taxis and hotels for journalists to write about their bands—and how this differed from the 'Cash For Questions' scandal that rocked the Westminster political landscape during the same period.

Of course, not all magazines and newspapers were so easily tempted, or, dare I say it, manipulated: over the years, I can distinctly remember offering several trips with several of my artists to several newspapers, and having to fight off their advances; not so the *Independent*.

'Would you like to come to New York to see * * * * * and write about them?' I once asked someone quite high up at that particular newspaper.

'No,' they replied. 'I am sorry, but we are independent—and we won't be bought.'

'That's fine,' I countered, 'so would you like to pay for the trip yourselves instead?'

'No,' they replied again. 'We can't afford it.'

At which point I sighed, no doubt in tandem with several hundred thousand otherwise independently minded readers not being able to read about their beloved Suede in their favourite newspaper for the foreseeable future.

infiltrates a band's after-show demeanour. The band's guitarist—and fifth mainstay, for that matter—Debbie Smith, seemed to be in a bit of a funk, so I sidled up next to her to see if I could cheer her up. Naturally, she was inconsolable, but she did reveal that she was finding the tour gruelling, as she couldn't work out whether she was the only lesbian in the whole of America. I tried to reassure her that she wasn't.

With the benefit of hindsight, I have to reassure my readers that I had no idea what I was talking about.

Everyone decided to go back to the hotel. I elected to share a car with Debbie so we could chat further. In the car, Debbie and I discussed whether we might accidentally end up at a late-night party where we would find evidence of lesbian activity—a prospect she considered as remote as discovering that aliens had been present in the dressing room prior to our arrival.

The car pulled up outside the Mondrian. As Debbie and I jumped out, I glanced around and saw that there was a long queue of people attempting to gain entrance to the hotel. The queue seemed to consist of glamorous women dressed in the kind of clothing and bouffant hairstyles you'd usually associate with the characters seen in 1980s TV shows like *Hart To Hart* or *The Love Boat*. When I examined the crowd in greater detail, I realised that there were no men in sight. Oh, actually, I lied, there was one: bewildered and confused, and seemingly lost in the queue, I spotted Johnny Depp.

I looked up at a flashing neon sign now hanging above the main entrance to the hotel—a sign I would certainly have remarked upon had it been there earlier that day.

Dallas And Dynasty Wives Night, it said.

Debbie and I looked at each other.

'Fuck me,' said Debbie. 'What the fuck is this about?'

What the fuck this was about was an actual fucking party being held for women who wanted to celebrate their love of *Dallas* and *Dynasty*, and possibly their sexuality, in equal measure. I stared at the sign for several minutes, wondering whether we had been dropped off at a sister hotel in an alternative reality all of our own bidding. I am almost certain that Debbie was as confused and dumbfounded as I was.

Debbie and I came to the momentous decision to check out the party. We were just about to join the queue when the hotel concierge beckoned us over to the hotel entrance: he had spotted the room key I had produced from my bag and now appeared insistent that we should be elevated to VIP status amongst the hoi polloi congregating outside the hotel. As we slipped by the concierge—our louche demeanour and gig-going attire had now persuaded the rest of the crowd that, as Joan Collins and Linda Evans had turned up, the queue was likely to move much more quickly—I nodded to the rest of the hotel staff, who acknowledged my presence as a resident of the highest order.

I could tell that Debbie was as reluctant to retire to her room as I was.

'Would you mind telling us where the party is happening in

the hotel?' I asked the young female member of staff I recognised from having brought me room service on a previous occasion.

'Yes, of course, madam,' came the reply. 'It's in the ballroom at the rear of the hotel, but you may have to change into something more appropriate to gain entrance to the party. There is a strict dress code, and ladies are expected to wear dresses or skirts, in accordance with the party's theme.'

For a moment, I was transported back to my teenage years when, after completing a round of golf with my best friend, I had attempted to gain access to the clubhouse of the rather old-fashioned golf club that presided—with a rod of four irons—over the management of the estate. My best friend had recently become traumatised by the fact that everyone we became acquainted with thought we were boyfriend and girlfriend, and when a pompous official confronted us on the doorstep to the clubhouse and insisted that I wouldn't be allowed in unless I wore a skirt, I sensed my friend's annoyance. Naturally, the affair was compounded when I took great delight in accepting the kindly chap's offer of borrowing one of the women's clubhouse skirts stored in the office for such eventualities. *Oh well,* I thought, *if that's your dress code then I embrace the sexist nature of your shitty club's policy and comply with your outrageous demands. And thank you, sir, for endorsing your club policy with such rigour and attention to detail.*

As for tonight's drama? Well, I would like to be able to tell you that the suitcase in my room was bursting at its seams with a selection of 1980s-influenced power-dresses and ballgowns

19

suitable for the purpose of transforming myself into the ravishing Texan housewife I'd no doubt always wanted to be. But, alas, no: Debbie and I made our way to the ballroom and took a look inside. It was packed to the rafters—and I did note the presence of rafters—with the most extraordinary selection of glamorous middle-aged women I had ever seen. We must have stood there for almost ten minutes, waiting for something to happen, before it didn't, and then we went back to our lives. Sometimes, things are just too good to be true.

* * *

If you were lucky enough to read my first book, *Lunch With The Wild Frontiers: A History Of Britpop And Excess In 13½ Chapters*, you may have noticed a brief reference to a party I attended with Suede in Paris in the mid 1990s. The party was notable for the fact that it took place after Suede had performed a triumphant show at a tiny venue called Passage Du Nord-Ouest on October 7, 1994. The short set featuring 'This Hollywood Life', 'We Are The Pigs', 'Killing Of A Flashboy', 'Animal Nitrate', 'Heroine', 'The Wild Ones', 'So Young', and 'Metal Mickey' marked the debut live appearance by the band's newest recruit, guitarist Richard Oakes, who had just turned eighteen, and the success of the show, and especially Richard's performance, ensured that everyone—and Brett in particular—was in extraordinarily fine spirits when they turned up at the unspeakably elegant apartment, finely situated within touching distance of the Eiffel Tower.

The apartment was owned by a well-known young French actress who went under the unlikely name of Taxi. At this point in our story, Taxi was starring in a popular soap series watched by enough people in her home country to make her presence on the Parisian social scene something of a notable phenomenon. Naturally, I can't remember how I ended up at her apartment, or indeed the ensuing party; I can only assume that I must have followed someone or other, after leaving the venue in a valiant attempt to ensure that several other members of Suede and their entourage—presumably we would have followed each other over several cliffs if we'd been asked to do such a thing, or so my mother would no doubt have suggested at the time—could be reunited with one another.

These days, when I come to think of the events of the evening—which is only every other day, when I am contemplating my existence as someone who neither owns an apartment within touching distance of the Eiffel Tower, nor is in a meaningful relationship with anyone who owns such a place—I remember Taxi spending most of the evening draped over Brett, a feat of romantic intertwining that was more than reciprocated by Brett himself. As to the historical, intimate details of how they knew each other? Well, I can only presume that Brett and Taxi had been acquainted for quite some time, and had perhaps become more of an item as a consequence of that evening's show; I have a distinct recollection of having met Taxi in the dressing room after the show, and, at one point, Brett shouting 'Taxi' in her general direction, which threw me for a while; I can only conclude that she may have made the decision to invite Brett and his sizeable entourage back to her apartment. *I must like you*, she might have said, at the time. *It doesn't even bother me that you come with this lot.*

When I arrived chez Taxi, I was immediately struck by the size and opulence of an apartment that had no right to be in such close proximity to one of the Seven Wonders of the World. Having said that, Taxi couldn't have been a more generous host, and she greeted me, and the unlikely assortment of likely characters that were now about to populate her apartment, with the kind of gentle bonhomie—you see how quickly I have warmed to my Gallic surroundings—that felt as genuine as it was no doubt unusual for someone of her standing.

The apartment had been created in such a way as to emphasise the character of each room—if any of my readers are sensing the presence of estate-agent parlance in my prose, then, in my defence, I would suggest that this is a direct result of the amount of that profession's inane jargon that has overwhelmed my letterbox, in pamphlet form, in recent years—and I was soon lost amidst a whirl of dining rooms and sitting rooms and the kind of kitchen that would have transported any realtor into a frenzy of anticipation for an impending sale.

That kitchen appeared to have been specifically designed for the purposes of ensuring that anyone lucky enough to find themselves standing around its central unit—carved out of the blackest and sleekest marble imaginable—would be torn between the obvious advantages afforded by the breath-taking views of the Eiffel Tower and the Champ de Mars, and the benefits provided by a surface capable of accommodating the consumption of cocaine. Of course, once one had chosen one thing over another, the evening nosedived spectacularly—or launched itself superbly, depending on one's views on the matter—into hapless oblivion: drugs were bought or exchanged before being consumed, and then all bets were off. I can remember wandering between four large living/dining room areas, each complete with a grand piano, before setting up shop in the most luxurious of these structures and attempting to play one of the pianos. Thankfully, several members of the rock band Suede quickly intervened before I could do any further damage to my reputation, but it was Brett who rushed to my aid, booting me off the piano stool and launching into a tinkling-the-ivories rendition of 'The Wild Ones', a track off the band's recently released second album, *Dog Man Star*—and 'the best Suede song ever' according to Brett himself—that was handily due to be released as a single the following month. Imagine his surprise when I immediately launched into a rendition of the first few verses of the song, replicating, in the finest detail, Brett's vocal technique to the extent that I could sense him thinking, *What is this monster that I have created?*

Of course, Brett should have known better: this *monster* had been created *sans sa participation*—I told you I was becoming good at this French lark—something I would have pointed out if I hadn't been so busy trying to impress the latest version of myself, which I was most happy with. Which is not to say that I was happy with any version of myself by this point in my life, just that I had been so intimately, romantically, and, for the sake of argument, professionally involved with Suede during the preceding three years that it felt as if I had some kind of divine right to express the intricacies of my obsession in the form of a 'Wild Ones' vocal tribute act bordering on a winning *Stars In Their Eyes* performance. And, if any of my readers are beginning to suspect that I had been rehearsing—is it called rehearsing when you are singing along to your favourite songs in front of your living room mirror?—with a view to an opportunity such as this to present itself, then they are mistaken.

Several hours later, after less appropriate marble surfaces had been utilised, everyone was draped over everyone else, and jocularity had ensued: by which I mean to say that, by this time, Brett and Taxi had disappeared into a bedroom, bassist Mat Osman and drummer Simon Gilbert were falling off chairs, and the band's latest wide-eyed recruit to join the ranks, (just-turned) eighteen-year-old guitarist Richard Oakes, was as wide-eyed as the rest of us. As the time approached 6am, and the din from Taxi's outrageously opulent stereo system reached cacophonous proportions, an ominously loud knocking could be heard coming from the apartment's front door.

Shamefully, tentatively, I found myself peeking around one of the living room doors when someone who probably should have known better beat me to it and rushed down the corridor to answer the front door. As it burst open—and I can't be entirely sure who was ultimately responsible for opening it—four members of the *Police nationale* burst into the apartment, shouting, 'What the fucking hell is going on? It's six o'clock in the morning and your music can be heard all the way down the Champ de Mars. Who is responsible for this?'

In actual fucking French.

I'd not seen a group of young men acting so violently since the Mary Chain brothers on the aforementioned *Rollercoaster* tour, and I was actually quite frightened. However, the bright spark who'd rushed to answer the front door had other ideas.

'Taxi,' he yelled, with all the urgency of someone hailing a cab in a rain-ravaged, war-torn district of Narnia.

'Taxi. TAXI!!'

The effect of his words was instantaneous. At the far end of the apartment, a door slid open, and a woman gently emerged into the dimly lit confines of the corridor. Naturally, it was Taxi, and as she sidled elegantly towards me—and, ultimately, towards the front door of her own apartment—I noticed her cream-colored, silk dressing gown, barely draped around her, held shut, or perhaps more likely held open, at the waist by a matching cream-colored, silk string belt of indeterminate expediency.

The four gentlemen of the law let out a collective sigh of relief, no doubt informed by a level of recognition that even I, at no small distance from proceedings, could recognise as, well, a bit of a *changeur de jeu*.

'Taxi!' they all shouted in unison.

Taxi smiled, and the four men from the *Ministry Against Fun* visibly crumbled in front of *Her Royal Soapstarryness*.

25

It is at this point in the narrative that I have to confess to certain inadequacies with regard to my understanding of the French language, although as Taxi and her newest and most important admirers continued to engage in animated conversation, I began to understand a little of what they were talking about: our erstwhile *enemies at the gate* now seemed overly keen on abandoning their evening shifts—is it still called an evening shift when it is six o'clock in the morning?—so that they could explore the possibility of joining the outrageous festivities that had brought their posse here in the first place. Taxi was having none of it, or so it seemed to me at the time, and ushered each one of them towards the door, exchanging intimate kisses on cheeks with all concerned, as if they were extended members of one another's households.

As soon as the *Police nationale* had left the premises—no doubt their official report on the evening's fun and frolics would have included the phrase *there was an incident in the early hours*—several members of the party decided to call it a night and head off home. And I decided to walk the streets of Paris on the lookout for illegal drinking dens. I ended up in the Pigalle and then, finally, and by midday, back at the hotel.

I was still sitting in the bar of the hotel—with several other members of the Suede posse—at two o'clock in the afternoon, when Brett sauntered in.

'*Hello Fruits!*' he said and sauntered off again.

2

HERE WE FUCKING GO

"In the morning, when I am making my way on foot to the festival site with Sam—Brett's girlfriend at the time—I remember me and Sam laughing as she is wearing a T-shirt sporting the slogan *No one knows my boyfriend is gay.*"

'*It's so formulaic, isn't it? The story of every band is exactly the same. Struggle, success, excess, disintegration.*'

The first thing you should know is that it is my birthday. I have spent the night before staying with the band in an unremarkable, slightly unloved hotel in the centre of Stratford Upon Avon, and I am far more nervous about Suede's headlining appearance the next day than anyone not actually in the band has any right to be. Phoenix is still a comparatively new addition to the festival circuit, and its inaugural appearance, two years previously, ended in carnage, and a riot of sorts, as festival goers vent their frustration at the enforced 10pm curfew—*plus ça change, plus c'est la même chose*, I hear you cry—and, whilst trying to exit the event, I get caught in the outpouring of manufactured grief and become quite terrified whilst several hundred drugged-up music aficionados start smashing up one of the walls surrounding the arena, subsequently using the bricks that come loose from the construction to break up further sections of the wall so that they can throw them at the security that try to stop them, and then finally each other.

Memories of the fracas are still upmost in my mind when I arrive at the hotel, but the first thing I remember is Simon telling me that, as he had been brought up in the area, he is slightly freaked out that he is now back to headline a festival, presumably on the very same common ground that he used to smoke fags on. And then, in the morning, when I am making my way on foot to the festival site with Sam—Brett's girlfriend at the time—I remember me and Sam laughing as she is wearing a T-shirt sporting the slogan *No one knows my boyfriend is gay.* Of course, no one knows who Sam is, or indeed who her boyfriend is, and as several magazines and newspapers have been trying to suggest that Brett is bisexual for several years, the T-shirt seems a cheeky, apposite response to this media conjecture.

I have several reasons to be nervous. When I announce Suede's appearance at the festival, I refer to them as headliners, even though Bob Dylan is on the same bill. Suede, their management, and indeed my PR company, Savage & Best, have always been insistent that the band will never play support ever again, presumably after they had to play second fiddle to vastly inferior pop fodder in their early days, but also because…well, why should they? They are now so vastly superior to everyone else currently knocking around the rock and pop landscape that there is no way they should have to suffer that ignominy again. I think the Stone Roses had the same idea, but let's times that by ten.

Once the press release has gone out, it is reproduced all over the music press and causes a bit of a stir. I immediately get a call from Dylan's PR people, who are apoplectic with rage that *His Holy Warbliness* has been relegated to second fiddle on the bill behind some 'Britpop' upstarts who presumably have only been releasing records for about five minutes. Inevitably, Suede's management have been receiving the same kind of calls, and a shared headline agreement surfaces on a new, carefully worded statement suggesting that the original billing had never been confirmed in the first place. Normal service is almost resumed.

The other reason I am nervous is that, as far as I can make out, this is the first time Suede are due to play in a live UK setting not entirely of their own choosing since the release of their second album, *Dog Man Star*, in October 1994. Of course, by my reckoning, they'd played around a hundred live shows all over the world since its release and perhaps four or five European festivals leading up to today's appearance, but this somehow feels different: the *Dog Man Star* UK tour earlier this year has been one of the most exciting tours I'd ever witnessed, but I am acutely aware that the cynicism engendered—in some quarters—by Bernard Butler's departure last year could translate to hostility in a public arena where they aren't preaching to the converted.

And then, ten minutes before Suede are about to take to the stage, the heavens open, and I think our time is up: this is apocalyptical stuff, the kind of downpour that would have cancelled proceedings if it had happened any earlier in the day. But it is too late: or, as a *Melody Maker* cover headline once screamed, 'Suedemania—it's too late to stop now.'

I am right at the front of the crowd—as I am at every Suede show I attend throughout the 1990s—and get the worst of the deluge due to the fact that the roof above the stage has collected more than enough rain water to drown anyone lucky enough to be as obsessed with Suede as I am. Naturally, I don't have a brolly, and when it sheds its load I am part of the cannon fodder the festival organizers have been waiting for. Within five minutes I am drenched to such an extent that I—and everyone else around me—am finding it funny. And then I hear 'Introducing The Band' and nothing else matters.

Brett looks amazing, and there's a white shirt and black tie and the kind of manicured fringe that looks effortlessly put together. But still, it's insane weather, and 'Heroine' starts and I genuinely think, *This is one of their dangerous songs . . . where's this going, then?* I can't figure out whether I was expecting 'This Hollywood Life' as usual, but Brett's fringe starts to disintegrate almost immediately, and you can see how it might now prove more of a hindrance than something you'd want to try at home. Then it's more danger with 'We Are The Pigs' and, yes, 'Metal Mickey' seems more urgent than normal, and when Simon starts the intro to 'Killing Of A Flashboy' it is incendiary, and suddenly I think, *I know what mood they're in.*

To the blessed and initiated, 'Killing Of A Flashboy' is, if not quite the best song of all time, then undoubtedly the best B-side of all time, and what I love about the song is that every time Suede perform it live and we all hear it, they know how effortlessly good it is, and we do too. And we know they know it's just about perfect, and they know we know it's just about perfect, and when Brett yells '*Here we fucking go*'—as he never does on the record— you know they're doing it just for you. Oh, and the sexy wiggle and the casual violence and the handclaps and that bit when the song stops in the middle for less than half a second before Brett sings, '*It's the same old show*' gets me every time.

31

'Animal Nitrate' is up next and completes the madness—by this time, Brett's hair has abandoned all attempts at being anything other than just something flapping around his head—and then there's respite of sorts with 'The Wild Ones' and 'By The Sea' before the cavalcade returns with 'The Drowners'—*How appropriate*, I remember gurgling at the time—and 'Together', and then 'The Asphalt World' is sublime enough to make me wish it was written about me but I know it wasn't, so maybe it's about you instead.

And then it all becomes a bit of a blur: I remember Brett swinging his hugely extended microphone lead around his head during the outro to 'So Young' and thinking, *This time someone's gonna get it in the head*, and then 'Daddy's Speeding' freaking me out, as it usually did, and 'My Dark Star' appearing out of nowhere, and suddenly it was all over. Oh, and did I mention the rain?

This is not meant to be a review, but guess what? Just as I feared, a journalist called Andy Gill reviews Suede's Friday night performance for the *Independent* newspaper and even suggests that the hubris surrounding the Suede/Dylan headlining mix-up had somehow caused the torrential downpour that precedes their set, almost as if it was an act of God and they got what they deserved. 'Poor old Suede,' he begins, but by the end of the review he is good enough to mention Brett's floppy fringe and that 'Brett is on a mission to inhabit the entire stage'—*Hello! Welcome to Suede!*— and that they just about get away with it. Well, as we all know, they more than get away with it, but what do newspapers know anyway. They don't even mention it is my birthday.

3

INTRODUCING THE BAND

❝If you really want to know anything about Suede's appearance at the Phoenix festival on July 14, 1995, you should be aware that it was the end of something and the beginning of something else entirely. We've all got to start somewhere, and this is as good a place as any.**❞**

*'It felt strangely apt that we were playing places like
Belgium and Holland, like weird deposed kings.'*

This book is primarily about Suede's third album, *Coming Up*, but
I make no excuses for naming this chapter after the opening track
on their second album, *Dog Man Star*. Nor do I apologise for
writing about a concert they performed fourteen months prior to
the release of *Coming Up* itself. Indeed, if you really want to know
anything about Suede's appearance at the Phoenix festival on July
14, 1995, you should be aware that it was the end of something
and the beginning of something else entirely. We've all got to start
somewhere, and this is as good a place as any.

Two years earlier—in March 1993 to be precise—Suede
released their eponymous debut album and, just for a moment,
the world went mad. In April the previous year, the band had
graced the cover of British rock weekly *Melody Maker*, although
they were yet to release a single, and found themselves catapulted
from obscurity to acclaim amidst the kind of hyperbole usually
reserved for kings and queens of tyrannical regimes. Naturally,
when *Suede* arrived almost a year later, the album went to no.1,
selling over 100,000 copies in its first week of release.

Suede went on to win the Mercury Music Prize, the band's
ubiquitous presence on the musical landscape—they graced
over sixty magazine covers in a three-year period—subsequently
redefining independent music as something to be celebrated
rather than side-lined. Suddenly, the leftfield had become the

mainstream—in 2015, the *NME* acknowledged this fact, awarding Suede its 'Godlike Genius Award' for 'fundamentally altering the course of alternative music in the 1990s'—and bands like Oasis, Blur, and Pulp could thank their lucky stars that a band like Suede *mattered* so much. And this despite the fact that two of these bands could hardly tolerate their existence.

Petty rivalries notwithstanding, Oasis and Blur in particular soon began to dominate a British music scene that frontman Brett Anderson, felt no affiliation with. 'I don't think anybody could deny that we pretty much kicked off what became Britpop,' said Brett over a decade later, 'and for a very limited time we were proud of that. Then everybody started singing about having a lovely bunch of coconuts and running up the apples and pears. It became horribly twisted, a musical *Carry On* film, and we did our utmost to distance ourselves from it.' They did indeed, and that 'whole boozy, cartoon-like, fake working-class thing' was swiftly side-stepped whilst the band went away to write *Dog Man Star*. Or as Brett puts it, ever more eloquently, 'You could not find a less Britpop record. It's tortured, epic, extremely sexual and personal. None of these apply to Britpop.'

The recording and release of *Dog Man Star* proved to be an abundance of mixed blessings. Whilst being hailed in some quarters as the band's masterpiece—the *NME*'s John Harris called it 'a startling record: an album surrounded by the white heat of something close to genius'—other critics, particularly in the US, saw it as pompous and overblown, and 'one of the most pretentious albums ever released by a major label'. The long player also facilitated the demise of the most gifted and lauded songwriting partnership since Morrissey and Marr. The album was recorded between March 22 and July 26, 1994, at Master Rock Studios in Kilburn, London, but that didn't stop guitarist Bernard Butler upping sticks and quitting the band on July 8. And yes, eagle-eyed readers will already have noticed that the dates don't match, and the record had yet to be completed.

Naturally, trouble had been brewing for quite some time. In early '94, when Suede were due to release their standalone single 'Stay Together', the band's spirits were at an all-time low: Butler's father had just died, and the band's second American tour appeared to be cursed by events beyond their control; the first week of the tour was cancelled, so they flew home early, and when the tour finally resumed, Bernard had started travelling separately from the rest of the band, sometimes on the tour bus of the support act. *That* support act was The Cranberries, who suddenly found themselves in the midst of a frenzy of US airplay on the back of their recent hit 'Linger'. The upshot of this ignominy, at least as far as Suede were concerned, was that The Cranberries leapfrogged Suede to headline status, and the last few dates were cancelled.

Meanwhile, back in the studio—or fast-forward to the studio, if you really want to be pedantic about it—Bernard had become convinced that Ed Buller's production was substandard and that he could do a better job himself. Latterly, Butler criticised the overall musicianship on the record, the lack of commitment in the studio, and the band's unwillingness to embrace his elaborate ideas. 'I just heard too many times, *No, you can't do that.* I was sick to death of it,' he said at the time. 'I think it's a good record, but it could have been much better.'

Butler had also started to find Anderson's increasing drug use problematic. 'I was doing an awful lot of acid at the time,' said Anderson, much later than required. 'We lived a pretty dissolute lifestyle. It was a mad blur of consumption. In between moments of hedonism, we'd stumble into the studio and write songs and I don't know how we managed to get anything done. Every day was crazy.'

Matters were compounded when Butler gave an interview to the July 1994 edition of *Vox* magazine—published in early June, a month earlier than the cover date, as is their wont—next to the headline 'Brett drives me insane'. The article proved to be the final nail in the coffin of Brett and Bernard's relationship—Butler went on to say, 'He's not a musician at all. It's very difficult for him to get his head around anything that isn't ABC'—and Brett can remember reading the article in Master Rock Studios whilst he was recording the vocals for 'The Asphalt World': 'I remember trying to channel all this hurt that I was feeling and the iciness I was feeling into the vocal.'

These days, Brett says that he always knew Bernard was going to leave, that there was always a kind of volatility around their relationship, but 'that's what made it exciting, the sense that it could all fall apart: that's what rock music is!' Presumably, he is referring to the fact that most members of finely tuned orchestral choirs or classical music quartets tend not to storm out of recording studios whilst shouting 'you're a fucking cunt' whilst spitting at each other, but he's also gracious enough to concede that Bernard's 'insane' comment concealed an element of truth. 'I am sure I drove everyone insane at the time,' he told DJ Chris Evans some twenty-five years later, 'but young men in their twenties, thrust into a position of power and wealth and privilege, and people telling them they are God's gift—that would drive everyone insane; it's a distortion of reality, it messes with your head.'

Whatever the truth of the matter, you should be aware that Suede barely *stumbled* towards an album release date that had been looming on my press schedule—here I should lay my cards on the table, and let you know that I was the band's publicist from 1992 until their initial split in 2003—for quite some time. Subsequently, the July 30 1994 issue of *Melody Maker* featured a Tom Sheehan photograph of Brett and Bernard that you just knew hadn't been posed for with the 'Is it all over for the best new band in Britain?' headline in mind—they had been snapped back-to-back, like gunslingers, on a previous encounter—and then it became ever more complicated: a few days after the *DMS* recording sessions, I set up a *Select* cover shoot with the band that was scheduled to appear in the magazine's October issue, but Suede were still a three-piece at this point, and attempts by photographer Rankin to snap all three remaining members in the same frame were summarily shunned; Brett was convinced that any band shot would make them look weak, or wounded somehow, like they were missing something.

Of course, what they were missing was Bernard—or a guitarist, at any rate—and when the magazine appeared a few weeks later, Brett stooped awkwardly on the cover amongst the tagline 'Suede: It all went horribly, horribly wrong. What the Butler saw'. Inside, there were no band shots to be seen, instead a mishmash of composite individual snaps and more accusatory bet-hedging, to wit: '3 unlimited: The Butler did it. Bailed out on Suede in a split that set a new record for acrimony. And the bitterness refuses to fade. If Brett, Mat and Simon stumble on the legal tightrope, it seems *Dog Man Star* might never come out at all.' It was all a bit *messy*.

On September 17, 1994, exactly two weeks after these comments appeared in print, Bernard was replaced by Richard Oakes, a seventeen-year-old guitarist from Poole in Dorset. Richard had submitted recorded versions of Suede songs—together with some of his own material—to the band's fan club, and as Brett revealed in Mike Christie's 2018 documentary *The Insatiable Ones*, 'I put the cassette in, expecting to be underwhelmed, and I wasn't. I heard this very eloquent, powerful, technically proficient guitar playing. It was the first time I'd heard someone play something of ours and really do the guitar part justice.' Indeed, when Simon originally heard Richard playing guitar whilst going through audition tapes, he mistakenly believed it to be an early Suede demo! But the cute ploy worked its magic—Richard beat five hundred other contenders for the role—and I immediately put out a statement confirming that he had answered an ad in the music press—just like Bernard—in an attempt to create the impression that it was business as usual, and seventeen-year-old guitarists always replace twenty-three-year-olds as part of the natural order of events.*

These days, Nude Records label boss Saul Galpern tells me that he should have been more concerned with Bernard's departure than he let on at the time. 'Of course, it crossed my mind that it could be over for the band in terms of continuing or even emulating the success they had achieved up to that point,' he says. 'But I had a strong belief in the band and Brett's confidence and determination. His desire was incredible; he can be so resilient with his focus.' Indeed, and despite Brett being wounded by what had happened, Saul sensed he wouldn't just give up. 'He never let his guard down in front of me,' he adds, 'and I was 100 percent with him and Mat and Simon, but I was aware that they were under the cosh: there was a feeling in the industry that they wouldn't get through this and the band were finished, but it was my duty as their label boss to support them.' Naturally, as Saul was kept abreast daily with the responses to *The Ad*—as it's come to be known around these parts—he became immediately aware of the excitement around Brett's discovery of the initial demo sent into Interceptor, Suede's management company, run by Charlie Charlton.

---

* In his second volume of autobiography, *Afternoons With The Blinds Drawn*, Brett hails Richard as 'the most naturally gifted musician I've ever worked with. He has an eerie ability to pick things out in music of which I'm simply not aware, let alone able to play'.

'On the day Richard was due to travel down for his audition in Elephant and Castle,' says Saul, 'I was told to be on stand-by. Then Brett called me and told me to drop everything and get my arse down there right away. *You got to hear this*, he said. And then, when I arrived at the rehearsal room, I couldn't quite believe my eyes. I did, in fact, think they'd found Bernard's double—going by the swagger, the look, and the performance. He could play all the songs note for note, maybe too technical and not as raw, but it must have been so daunting for the kid. I remember the relief and intensity in the room that day. It really did feel like a special moment, and, from that moment on, the atmosphere changed around everyone.'

In *Love And Poison*, David Barnett's excellent 2003 biography of Suede, Richard remembers performing 'Metal Mickey' during his audition and Brett kicking over his mic stand because he was so excited, but 'I still didn't think they'd ask me to join'. History now suggests that they did and the appointment couldn't have proved more timely, as the vultures had already begun to swoop. The day before the announcement, the *Guardian* newspaper, whilst admitting that lead single 'We Are The Pigs'—a superbly realised slice of recalcitrant non-pop—was 'one of their best', also predicted it would be the band's swansong, and when Richard made his first public appearance with Suede at the *Top Of The Pops* studio on September 22—can you imagine that?—he'd only been an official member for a grand total of five days. The poor thing had to mime Bernard's guitar parts to the song. Heads were scratched, but I'd love to know what people were expecting him to do.

41

Richard tells me that his *Top Of The Pops* appearance was 'amazing', although it felt 'very surreal to be appearing on a show I had been watching my whole life. I still felt like I had won some sort of competition, as opposed to embarking on a serious career. It felt a little silly miming when I had been hired for my actual playing ability, but it was still fun to be there and realise how small it is in real life. And that was before we'd even played a gig, so it was my first experience of standing on a stage, being sized up by the small TV audience and the millions of people watching at home. Before that point, I don't believe I had ever been judged on my own appearance. It was a totally new experience, and one I've never really been able to equate with being a musician.'

Mat Osman later described the decision to release 'We Are The Pigs' ahead of 'The Wild Ones' as 'commercial suicide', and I can't help thinking that Brett must have felt he could get away with releasing any old dark (admittedly brilliant) nonsense and it would be a hit. The song is about 'revolution and the juxtaposition between the middle-class lives of Highgate'—where Brett was living at the time—'and the council estates of Archway', but when he heralded it as 'a warning to the middle classes that everyone they're keeping under their feet is going to end up crushing their skulls. It's supposed to be quite a violent thing', you began to think, *He's not fucking joking.* Not even the inclusion of the superb *Dog Man Star* reject 'Killing Of A Flashboy'—I think I've already said enough about this superb, *Clockwork Orange*-tinged glam rocker—on the B-side could prevent the record peaking disastrously at no.18.

To all intents and purposes, 1994 was shaping up to be Suede's *annus horribilis*, as, by the time *Dog Man Star* came out, Blur's *Parklife*, released in April that year, was happily ensconced in its ninety-week stint inside the UK album charts and beginning to sell forty thousand copies a week. To make matters worse, Oasis's debut album, *Definitely Maybe*, had finally appeared in August and was now threatening to eclipse all so-called competitors in its wake. Never had the expression *bigger boys came* seemed more appropriate, or more damning.

Despite several protestations that the game was up, Suede shook themselves down and carried on. On October 10, 1994, the day *Dog Man Star* was due to be released, Richard made his first full UK live appearance at a secret fan-club show at London's Raw Club—three days earlier, he'd appeared on stage at the Passage du Nord-Ouest in Paris—and thus kicked off a series of around thirty-seven shows that would see the band through to the new year. Richard was a sensation, but I can't pretend that this wasn't one of the strangest periods in the band's tumultuous history: on the first leg of their European tour, Suede were accompanied by the Manic Street Preachers, who had just released *The Holy Bible* and were going through a few problems of their own. For the record, Suede and the Manics were mutual admirers—the latter had already covered 'The Drowners'—and Brett felt a kinship because 'we were going through similar periods of our career. The whole cartoon Britpop world was just starting to happen, and it felt like we were exiles.' It didn't seem to matter that every gig was incendiary; the sense that the band just wanted to move on to the next stage of their lives was *palpable*—and every time they tried to move on, Bernard was there to haunt them. Nevertheless, in the January 14 1995 edition of the *NME*, the main issues of the day were addressed with the coverline, 'Beat on the Brett: Is it all too much for Suede?', slapped on top of an early morning portrait of Brett (on Primrose Hill) by Kevin Cummins—'I'd been up all night, that seemed somehow unfair,' Brett admitted in a TV interview eighteen months later—and it all seemed like a witch-hunt.

Richard now describes this episode in his life as being 'like a leap off a cliff into the unknown. I had almost no experience of life outside of school/family, had dedicated my teenage years to learning to play and write, not even leaving time to be a rebel. There was so much media attention on Bernard quitting Suede and the build-up to the release of the *difficult second album*. Once I got the job, I realised I was going to be thrust into the limelight and that everyone would focus solely on my age and lack of experience. I'm not at all an extrovert so I had to sort of build some psychic defences against the attention in a very short time. I remember people saying to me that they couldn't believe I was so sensible and down-to-earth, taking it all in my stride, but the truth is that it was such a huge thing happening to me, and such a complete change of circumstances, that if I had allowed myself to focus on the bigger picture, I would probably have gone insane. Every single detail of my life changed completely overnight. So, I closed my eyes as you might do on a rollercoaster. I honestly don't

44

think the magnitude of it hit me properly until we had started recording *Coming Up*. But I was protected from the worst of it by the other members of the band and especially Charlie, who I was staying with at the time. I feel they were cautious about how young I was, despite the fearlessness they presented to the press.'

Despite Richard's protestations, his spell lodging with Charlie Charlton, the band's manager for most of the 1990s and beyond, lasted a mere few weeks before he started staying in a spare room provided by Mike Christie in his Mossford Street house in Mile End. Christie, a young filmmaker who'd become part of Suede's inner circle after he introduced his close friend and work colleague Derek Jarman to the band back in April 1993, felt like a perfect fit for a lengthier domestic arrangement: Christie had recently made an experimental film for 'The Asphalt World' and was due to be going on the first leg of the *Dog Man Star* tour, so it made sense that he and Richard could come and go together.*

On January 30, 1995, the band released 'New Generation', the third single from *Dog Man Star*, and the signs were good: the flipside proudly sported Richard's first co-writing credits, including the gently cascading, midtempo, Bowie-esque ballad 'Bentswood Boys' and 'Together', the latter showcasing a monstrous guitar riff reminiscent of Buzzcocks' finer moments. Christie remembers Richard coming home from the studio with

---

* At this initial meeting, Jarman was approached with a view to directing a video for 'So Young'; he ended up providing his films as a backdrop for Suede's Clapham Grand show on July 12, 1993.

the DAT for 'Together'—'even though Brett hadn't finished the lyrics and had *miaowed* over the end'—and 'playing it over and over again, more excited than I've ever seen him before or since'. Richard reveals that, before 'Together' appeared, 'We had already written a batch of songs in late '94, including "Have You Ever Been This Low" and "Young Men", and the bones of what would eventually become "Picnic By The Motorway", but "Together" and "Bentswood Boys" came from an evening in Hamburg when the others went out drinking but I still felt too young for that, so I stayed in, watched German TV, and strummed around for ideas. The legend is that I was locked in a hotel room until I came up with some songs, but that's not true.'

Happily, Richard is not surprised that I can hear a Buzzcocks influence on 'Together', as the band were hugely influential on him when he was first learning to put songs together at the age of thirteen and fourteen. He also reveals that 'Together' was an old song called 'Outside' by his former band TED that he'd embellished with 'new bits', and 'Bentswood Boys' was a simple set of chords that Brett liked. 'I never demoed them,' he says now. 'They found their form when we recorded them at Wessex Studios in December 1994: "Together" became a big, brash, swinging glam-pop song and "Bentswood Boys" a much more reflective piece, and I loved the imagery Brett came up with when singing about his origins. I was fiercely proud of both songs, and to record them in a studio where some of my favourite ever music was recorded—I remember rehearsing while sitting on the drum riser used for the stomps on

"We Will Rock You" and thinking, *OMG*—was just brilliant. And the sense of relief other people had when they heard them. Many people around the band approached me and said, *Well done, we knew you could do it*, but I could see the relief in their faces.'

In October 2021, on the eve of Suede's *Coming Up* twenty-fifth-anniversary tour of the UK, Ed Buller told *Guitar* magazine's Andy Price, 'Richard was very needed in a way. It wasn't until the success of *Coming Up* that the rest of the band thought, *Fuck me, we lucked out there*.' Saul Galpern is perhaps even more bullish when he tells me that Richard was like 'a raw footballer, pushed into the main team, expected to develop and perform'. Having said that, it turned out to be the perfect apprenticeship, since he could go on tour for six months, get to know what it was like being in Suede, and have some amazing experiences across the world, as well as learning the songs and working out how to write songs for the future. 'There was some evidence growing that Richard could co-write,' says Saul, 'and Brett worked hard to coax it out of him. "Together" and "Bentswood Boys" were an indication of a future, post-Bernard, but as good as they were, those songs were always meant to be B-sides.'

Subsequently, the video for 'New Generation' would feature Richard 'miming' Bernard Butler's guitar parts, so you could be forgiven for thinking we were back to square one. But fear not: the *Dog Man Star* tour was continuing apace, and Richard was coming to terms with a new reality where he was the best new guitarist in the best new band in Britain. 'At first, it didn't feel at all strange to be playing someone else's material,' he tells me. 'It was the one thing I knew I could do well, so the first batch of gigs were just a fun party where I got to impress everyone. But as the tour went on, it did become frustrating; slogging all the way through "Asphalt World" night after night became dull for everyone. I remember a gig in Italy in late '94 when, after the end of it, we broke into "My Old Man's A Dustman", which was as much of a dig at Blur as it was to relieve the monotony. I remember when we started to play "Together" live, it'd be the moment in the set I looked forward to most, and it reflected the band we were becoming perfectly. It crackled with a new energy and attitude. Suede had stopped being the dark goth overlords of indie and had, at least for a while, turned into a punk band.'

The UK leg of the *DMS* tour culminated in two shows at the Hammersmith Palais on February 6 and 7; by the time the band arrived at the Phoenix festival in July, they'd played eighteen different UK and Ireland shows, as well as fifty-nine further dates around the globe, including thirteen in the USA and eight more in Japan. By all accounts—hey, I didn't go to all of them—every show was a triumph, but it's testament to the band's *sangfroid* that, by the end of the tour, they were performing a set they had surely fallen out of love with a long time ago. Indeed, when I think back on those extraordinary series of dates, I may as well be looking back at some old footage of Concorde taking off in the 1980s—a glorious, long-forgotten glimpse of a lost future, a proud beast pushing up against the clouds.

4

GET INTO BANDS AND GANGS

> **"**Of course, there's an elephant not yet in the room, and his name is Neil Codling.**"**

'It was a chance to do everything Dog Man Star didn't
and make a bright, communicative album. It's like a
pendulum: you go one way and then the other.'

In January 1997, four months after the release of *Coming Up*,
Brett told *Melody Maker*, 'I tend to be quite optimistic about stuff
and drag the rest of the band through, but most of 1995 was
a terrible low point that I wouldn't want to go back to. It was
never a case of jacking it in, but there were a lot of doubts in my
mind about whether we could make a decent album. 'Cos you
know Bernard left the band and I couldn't be sure we could just
pick it up again. I know that with Bernard it was a really special
band. That's something you can't just dismiss and say it'll be all
right. I may be confident but I'm not that confident. Losing a key
member like that, there's a chemistry that's been destroyed.'

Correspondingly, as the band's Phoenix skirmish blended into
recent memory, Brett confirms that 'it was becoming really not
much fun touring an album that wasn't made by the band and
in many ways felt irrelevant to us'. A new album was, therefore,
very much forming in his mind during the *Dog Man Star* tour,
but 'those were quite dark times for me. It felt that the media had
had their heads turned by other bands. Even though that period
was frustrating, it was necessary. Richard was still very young, and
that tour helped him assimilate and acclimatise. The endless dead
hours rattling along autobahns and motorways listening to music
together in the back of the bus was invaluable and essential to the

identity of the album that was forming in our heads. I realised very early on that it would be ridiculous to try and compete with the grandeur and scope of *Dog Man Star*—that the white-hot energy of that album was unique to the strange, intense crucible in which it was made and that the only way forward was to go in a completely different direction.'

Richard maintains that 'Phoenix was a strange one, a big deal—being the last performance of the tour, being on TV, and sharing a bill with legends such as Bob Dylan—but it also felt like the comfy transition period was over, and now we'd have to get on with writing a follow up to *Dog Man Star*, so there was going to be immense pressure on me. I tried to not look at it too closely at that point, we had already written a few songs and I felt as though I had a handle on how to write with Suede, but being on tour for so long, staying either on people's sofas or on a tour bus . . . it felt as if I had been in constant motion since the day I joined. After the tour ended, I had my own flat in Westbourne Grove, got given an eight-track recorder, and suddenly life calmed down and became quiet. I had to learn to live alone in London as well as write an album!

'The magnitude of the task didn't really hit me until we were actually recording. I wasn't exactly sure what sort of album we were going to write . . . all I knew at that point was that it would be distilled and streamlined and hit you hard. We had a lot of punk ethics at the time; we were always listening to Sex Pistols and playing their songs at soundchecks and occasionally at gigs.

I believe it was a natural reflex against what Suede had gone through recording *Dog Man Star*, and it fitted in with my musical tastes and upbringing perfectly. But I didn't have a clear idea of the actual sonic feel of the new album until we wrote "Filmstar" and "She".'

On the eve of *Coming Up*'s release, in an *NME* cover story that thrusted and parried as if the magazine's life depended on it, Brett reflected on Richard's appointment thus: 'It seems insane in retrospect, judging someone simply on their ability to play someone else's guitar lines. But I trust my instincts and it all clicked together well. He didn't have much drive at first but being on that *Dog Man Star* tour and seeing everyone's misconceptions put a lot of fire in his eyes.'

Brett was in more reflective mood when interviewed in the August 1996 edition of *Vox* magazine. 'It's difficult when you're playing some bloody festival in Finland,' he said in the offending article, 'and you're knocking out the old tracks and you're just thinking, *Fucking hell, I can't wait to get back home, and carry on writing, because I've got it inside me to come back and write a fucking great album*. As soon as the songs started to flow, you knew there was something incredibly exciting on the horizon.'

'As soon as we came off that tour,' Brett says, 'we threw ourselves into the writing with a kind of crazed zeal.' Saul Galpern maintains that Brett needed a co-writer to bounce off—someone who could inspire him—and it was unfair to imagine a scenario where he might fill Bernard's shoes. Of course, in retrospect, Richard 'has proved his worth many times over,' says Saul now, 'and it's fair to say that without his simple, hooky riffs and style of playing, *Coming Up* would have been a very different sounding record.'

Brett is also adamant that Richard's taste in music, and the fact that he was younger than the rest of the band, 'suggested that we should make something charged and nimble—something that felt exactly like what in many ways would be another debut album.' We'd guessed as much, but a move from Highgate to Chesterton Road in west London ultimately put more of a spring in his step.

'The last album was very specific in terms of the way I wrote it,' Brett told *Vox* on the eve of *Coming Up*'s release. 'I rented a house in Highgate, it was this old Victorian Gothic gaff. It was this flat in this house. And the rest of the house was owned by this strange set of Christians called Mennonites. I had this studio to write in, didn't ever see anyone because no one could be bothered to come to Highgate. So I started writing in a very isolated way. We drove past the house the other day and Richard was in the car and I said, "Look there's my old house, that's where I wrote the whole of the last album," and he goes, "It reeks of *Dog Man Star*." And it did. It was this kind of dark, classical place.'

Indeed, if it could be said that the first version of Suede was brooding and Byronic and poetic, then I suppose it could also be said that the next version of the band—the one that spawned *Dog Man Star*—was a tortured and sprawling bastardisation of something that barely resembled its previous incarnation. 'We

53

couldn't go there mentally again,' says Brett, ''cos *Dog Man Star* was a fractured process and so unpleasant to make. We wanted to be in a room and enjoying playing together.'

Thankfully, as if to disagree with my original assessment— of two versions of Suede before *Coming Up*—when asked if the arrival of *Coming Up* marked the arrival of Suede Mk2, and whether the first two albums were part of Suede Mk1, Brett reflects, 'We've been lucky, 'cos we have had at least two debut albums.' By which I think he means to say that *Coming Up* was so different to anything they'd released before that it has to be assessed as a standalone record. He also maintains that it's 'a cartoon, day-glow kind of a record' and that they haven't made anything like it since.

As Brett began to write the new album 'back where I've always lived in London, in Ladbroke Grove'—where 'it reeks of the new album and is more part of real life'—a new philosophy began to emerge: the next Suede record would feature 'ten hits'. Mat Osman had hinted at this change of direction in *Select* magazine the previous year, or at least he'd suggested that he wanted to move on from the regimented recording process and expansive multi-layered guitar sounds of the *Dog Man Star* era and focus on more radio-friendly pop music. He'd cited R.E.M.'s 'Losing My Religion' as a song that 'doesn't show off in the slightest and is still brilliant'. Ed Buller was just as effusive on the subject: 'We wanted to make Michael Jackson's *Thriller*.'

Talk about setting the bar high.

Brett had a tiny, soundproofed writing room in his flat, and he remembers 'countless afternoons there, sweating and shrieking into my microphone searching for that special moment, that slither of songwriting alchemy that is so elusive but so worth the chase'. But he also recalls spending that summer wandering round to Richard's flat in Kensington Gardens Square and sitting down on his sofa bed and writing. In fact, both 'She' and 'Filmstar' came about through Brett bringing along a very simple line and slapping his hands on his knees to approximate a rhythm whilst Richard improvised and intertwined a guitar part. Here, the pair would spend 'endless nights which faded into sunny mornings, sitting by the gas fire, listening to records, strumming and singing'—a process presumably a million miles away from 'the dank, tortured neurosis' of the previous album.

Of course, there's an elephant not yet in the room, and his name is Neil Codling. Codling had witnessed Suede's incendiary performance at Phoenix–a festival held at Long Marston Airfield, just down the road from where he and his cousin, Simon Gilbert, spent their youth. 'In the 1980s, I used to play cricket with Bruce, the guy who managed the airfield,' he says now, 'and he'd rent it out for Girl Guides tea parties. The Bulldog Bash rally was held there every August, but Phoenix was more eclectic than biker bands. It was odd to have Bob Dylan and Public Enemy coming to play a festival stage five miles from where I grew up.'

Neil remembers Phoenix as being a pretty triumphant show, despite the rain and the rumbling row with Dylan. 'There was a glimpse of new material—"Together", "Young Men", and "By The Sea" with Richard on piano—and there was a definite end-of-term feel to it: a sense of a line being drawn.' He agrees that there was an air of celebration that the band had got through the *Dog Man Star* tour intact and unscathed, but that the work would soon have to begin if they were to carry on and convince anyone they were still contenders.

The story of how Neil came to join Suede 'by osmosis' has become part of the folklore surrounding the band. The short, received version is that in early autumn '95, as the band were cantering through rehearsals at the Church, Dave Stewart's recording studio in Crouch End, Neil, a recent graduate—with a 2:1 in English and Drama—from Hull University, popped in to see Simon, ostensibly to ask if he could borrow a suit for a job interview. At some point or other, Neil started messing about with various instruments—a method of engagement that proved impressive enough to make Brett and the rest of the band sit up and take note.

Correspondingly—and if you really want to get to the heart of the matter—you should know that Neil had already moved to Crouch End with his friend Jim as early as July that year, a week after graduating early from university. Neil and Jim began by renting two tiny rooms in an attic in Rathcoole Gardens, just around the corner from Konk Studios. At this juncture in his recently acquired independent status as a north London resident, Neil was surviving on dole handouts of £35 per week. A day's food would be half a vegan pie from the Haelan Centre, a health-food shop nestled in the heart of Crouch End.

'I smoked roll-ups with the cheapest tobacco I could get my hands on, Cutters Choice,' he tells me. 'A friend from college lived above a laundrette on Crouch End Hill. One of her flatmates had a sheet of purple microdots that were £2 each. They were a cheap way to get off our heads and keep the hunger pangs at bay for a good while. I told Simon about the acid, and he invited me round to his place on Portobello Road to take it with him and hang out. While I was there, Brett popped round for something and asked me, *Are you tripping?* and I said I was. He knew me as Simon's cousin—as a schoolboy, later student, who came to see Suede shows and hung around backstage like a lot of people back then—but here I was more of a mate or a peer.'

Church Studios in Crouch End was the first proper recording studio Neil had ever been in, so he 'had a good nose around, played on some instruments and listened to some of the stuff the band were working on. That was when they saw I was a musician.'

Saul Galpern remembers turning up at the Church Studios one morning when the band were all hanging out doing some demos, and Neil was hanging around too.

'He was introduced to me as Simon's cousin,' says Saul. 'And I had no idea what was to follow. Gradually, his name kept being mentioned, and the next thing Brett said that Simon had failed to mention he was a keyboard player and a trained musician. I think Brett liked Neil's instinctive observations. Even though his musical input was minimal at this stage, I think Neil had really cool touchstones of taste that had an influence.'

'I hung out some more that late autumn,' Neil clarifies. 'We'd have a drink, take this and that, listen to music, and acoustic guitars would come out. As important as any audition was whether I got on with the guys in the band. They asked if I could pop down to a rehearsal at Backstreet under the arches on the Holloway Road at the end of October and play along to some of the songs they'd written for *Coming Up*. They gave me a tape of some of the new songs the day before, and I stayed up and learned the parts and the vocal harmonies. We played things like "Lazy", and I sang the harmony in the chorus, and everyone said it sounded just like the record, even though there was no record to speak of at the time.'

When they first met, Richard recalls Neil playing the piano and noticing he had 'sign on:' scrawled on the back of his hand. Richard knew instinctively that Neil was a good musician, but it was also pretty apparent that Neil was akin to a Suede song made flesh. Brett remembers knowing 'immediately that he should be part of the band', and soon Neil was providing second guitar and backing vocals—a natural development that led to him joining. 'We were a family, a gang again,' said Brett at the time, 'a hormonal, rowdy leather-clad gang wreathed in the smoke of too many Benson & Hedges.'

A little while later, on January 27, 1996, that 'gang' was miraculously unveiled at a secret fan-club show at the Hanover Grand in London. The show marked the moment when Neil officially joined Suede, but the nine-song set drew another very important line in the sand: featuring 'She', 'Beautiful Ones', 'Together', 'Picnic By The Motorway', 'By The Sea', 'Filmstar', 'Lazy', 'Saturday Night', and 'Young Men', the reinvigorated line-up's short but vital clutch of new material dispensed with Butler tunes altogether, prompting the *NME* to conclude it was 'a set that says *no need*'. Indeed, such was the gang's newfound confidence that it would be many months before they deigned to reintroduce some of the pre-Oakes oldies back into their live act.

Richard recalls 'getting to know Neil a bit in summer 1995 from him coming round to Brett's for a party or going out boozing with us, and he was definitely one of the gang in his attitude, music tastes, and humour. I was also aware from early on that he was a songwriter and could play piano and guitar. It felt weirdly natural for him to start tinkling along with us at rehearsals and demo sessions. He was into what we were doing, and also it was good fun for me to have someone in the fold who was a little closer to my age.'

The last official engagement that Suede fulfilled without Neil in tow was a cover of Elvis Costello's 'Shipbuilding' for the War Child charity album, *Help*, in September 1995, but by the time the band started recording *Coming Up* at the Townhouse three months later, he had become a proper member. 'It was a gradual process over a few months,' says Richard, 'and I am not sure if he got a formal invite! He introduced a new musical chemical into what we were doing; he had a keen sense of pop and was into people like Scott Walker and The Fall. *Coming Up* would have been a very different album if he hadn't joined. But I think, ultimately, it did take some of the pressure off me, and even more so when the album actually came out and we were in the public eye again. Neil had a natural sense of presentation and how to be a pop star, which I didn't at all—when I first joined, the band hated my clothes and I had to be literally dressed up to look like a generic member of Suede—so I was happy for him to step forward for Suede's new image and let me step back a bit.'

Neil now suggests that some of the people around the band—Charlie and Saul, perhaps—didn't know what to make of him at first, so any excitement on his part was tempered by their mood. 'As you know,' he tells me, 'bands then were so at the mercy of the inky rock press that you really couldn't rely on an income or plan far into the future.' Neil remembers that a few weeks after he'd started going along to rehearsals at Backstreet, Brett asked him if he'd like to be a part of the band. 'By that stage it felt like the next step, rather than a momentous moment,' he says. 'I was twenty-one and had the lack of fear that comes at that age and just took it all as it came along. I was scraping by and was still very new to London, so although the band stuff happened quite fast, it was offset by the mundanity of sitting around in a dingy flat, wondering if it'd all work out. I was a realist, and I didn't expect to be an integral part of the band: the Manics had a keyboard player, but he was in the shadows behind the amps on stage. Rob from Supergrass played on the records but never appeared in photoshoots.'

Of course, as soon as Neil found himself standing right on the lip of the stage at the Hanover Grand, he realised that he might not be destined to be just another hired gun in the background. The *NME*'s Steve Sutherland described Neil's appearance that day as 'sulky, skinny and dead-eyed as a fashion model, hands on hips, the occasional backing vocal, a pouty threat from a clockwork orange, an occasional pianist, an immobile show stealer'. For my part, he reminded me of a slightly less animated and impossibly good-looking version of Ron Mael, Sparks' improbably odd-looking keyboard player.

These days, Neil is humble enough to let on that 'Brett and the band must've seen something in me'. And then, ever more graciously, 'Just about anyone can sing along and play rhythm guitar and simple piano parts. I could see and hear how talented Richard was and knew that the band could work as a four-piece. My strength is filling in the gaps, playing whatever else needs to be played on any given song. Having an extra body in the room gave a touch more width and scope to the sound of the band in rehearsal. We could work on arrangements beyond the drums/bass/guitar formula. I suppose I looked the part too. I was seven and a half stone and smoked like a chimney, so I fitted right in.'

Seven and a half stone! Maybe I should think again about that *Suede song made flesh* line.

* * *

On the eve of *Coming Up*'s release, Brett would tell the *Daily Telegraph*'s Neil McCormick that he'd wanted the record to be 'a complete turnover from the last album, which was very dark and dank. I wanted it to be almost like a *Greatest Hits*, the sort of album you could listen to at low volume, with pop songs on it that gradually bore their way into your head.' Perhaps more revealingly, in what can only be seen as a shrug of indifference in the general direction of his musical career to date, he also suggested, 'The first two albums suffered from being at certain times quite obscure. I wanted it to be communicative and understandable. Pop music generally has to be pretty dumb, I think.' And then, with a dismissive nod towards *Dog Man Star* in particular, 'I've had my little affair with the avant-garde. It's not as exciting as pop music.'

Initially, Ed Buller, who had produced the band's previous two albums, was not the first choice to produce the new record. Brian Eno (who'd previously worked on a version of 'Introducing The Band' that ended up as the flipside of 'The Wild Ones'), Flood, Steve Lillywhite, John Leckie, and Chris Kimsey were among several candidates investigated, but their schedules proved irreconcilable. Even Chris Thomas, who'd wanted to work with Suede prior to their first album, and Scott Litt, famed for his work with R.E.M., were considered at one stage. Saul Galpern admits that, when he was sending out demos of songs such as 'Money' and 'We're So Disco'—later to be B-sides—he didn't really know what kind of record he had on his hands. Brett was particularly enamoured of 'Money', suggesting to Saul that it was one of the best things he'd ever written and that it was going to be a huge hit. 'I think it was the first post-Bernard song Brett played me,' says

Saul, 'but I was underwhelmed and just thought, *You can do better on every level.*'

Eventually, more by accident than design, and after a series of meetings, Buller found that his ideas about a new Suede direction tallied almost exactly with the band's own: to write less complex, more immediate songs; to use heavier drum sounds, play fewer guitar solos, and only employ string sections when absolutely necessary. 'It was actually a relief when we went back to Ed,' adds Saul, 'as he was the only one who wouldn't stand for mediocrity. He really understood the band and I think because he understood the history, the influences and the aesthetics, he could help nurture Richard in particular.'

Ed was always 'very much the Fifth Beatle in Suede', Brett says now. 'But it was interesting to see his role change between the first two records and *Coming Up*. I think when Bernard left, Ed sensed that there was a vacuum which needed to be filled in order that the band could operate properly in the studio, and I think he decided to take the reins a little, steering the ship and nudging the music towards his own personal vision of what the band could be.'

Whilst acknowledging Brett's comments on 'steering the ship', it's just as important to acknowledge that *Coming Up* marked the first time that Ed had had to address Brett's dominating personality—or, if you will, his *presence*. 'Every band should have a front man,' says Ed, 'and not every band does, but just before we went into the studio, I told Brett he wasn't going to like every idea on the record, it wasn't just about him, and I was going to fight for the others, particularly Richard.' All well and good, you might think, but perhaps Ed's newly forged strategy of standing up to Brett should be seen as an ongoingly weary response to the band's historically difficult interpersonal relationships. No doubt you are sensing an ongoingly weary reticence on my part to address such a subject, but when you consider that Ed had spent the last five years watching the most celebrated singer/guitarist collaboration of the 1990s disintegrate before his eyes, you will forgive me— and perhaps even him—for such conjectures.

As if to illustrate my hypothesis, Ed tells me that the first time he noticed any acute tensions between Brett and Bernard was whilst Suede were recording the B-sides to 'Stay Together'—the magnificent 'My Dark Star' and 'The Living Dead'—and Bernard began to insist on turning all the vocals down. I am assured that this became more of a Bernard-induced common practice during the *Dog Man Star* sessions, with the result that Brett wasn't able to figure out how his vocals could fit in amongst the cacophony of guitars now emanating through his headphones. This was surely Bernard's intention, but *The 'Stay Together' Incident* proved to be a turning point of sorts: after the band had 'nailed' it—I believe that some of the more insistent rock critics and even some of the more insistent rock groups choose to refer to a band's successful completion of their recording activities in this way—they went to the pub, sans Bernard, and Ed mentioned that he thought he had let Brett down.

'Yes, you did let me down,' said Brett. 'You stood with Bernard. But then you always stand with Bernard.'

Inevitably, I am toying with the embroideries of such an exchange, although I have to confess that it would be impossible for any of my own highly emotionally charged recollections of the to-and-fros of the era to substantially contradict any of Ed's more numerous and, perhaps, more intimately realised encounters: indeed, when I ask Ed whether *The 'Stay Together' Incident*—see how the phrase now seems to have taken on a life of its own— had influenced any further band-producer interactions, he is quite adamant that it was a precursor to him standing up to Bernard during the *Dog Man Star* sessions. Which begs the question: if Ed hadn't noticed that Bernard was trying to dominate Brett during the 'Stay Together' recordings, and then brought the subject up, would Brett have ever brought the subject up himself? And now that Ed has confirmed that Bernard initiated all the confrontations in the studio—presumably every other confrontation was initiated by Brett's drug activities and a decadent lifestyle that Bernard found abhorrent?—do we all agree that Bernard meant for these confrontations to lead to him and Brett falling out for ever? And could a record like *Coming Up* ever have existed without the split that preceded it?

Whatever the truth of the matter, 'Ed always saw Suede as a much more—for want of a better phrase—70s-sounding band than I think we actually really were,' says Brett. 'The rough, jagged edges that a band like us will always have were often sanded down in his pursuit of a kind of pop sensibility. Sometimes I regret this—something like "Metal Mickey", for example, would have been better as a nasty punk song—but generally it worked, and the pop sheen of *Coming Up* was very heavily influenced by Ed's tastes.'

In an explicit act of concurrence, Ed suggests that the early 70s work of T. Rex was a major influence on the sound of the album. Certainly, the band have admitted immersing themselves in T. Rex's 1972 masterpiece *The Slider* and, thanks to Saul Galpern, its follow-up, *Tanx*. 'Everyone goes on about *Electric Warrior* and *The Slider*,' says Saul now, 'and they're obviously great records. But I gave Brett a copy of *Tanx*, and he absolutely loved it.' Ed maintains that he wanted to make the record 'the *Slider* of the 90s', and so T. Rex became the blueprint of the recording process.

Coming Up was recorded between December 1995 and June 1996 at several different locations, although Ed remembers that one of the overriding driving forces for their choice of studio was that they shouldn't return to Master Rock in Kilburn, as it shared such affiliations with *Dog Man Star*. Naturally, Master Rock eventually ended up as one of the venues for *Coming Up*'s recording activities further down the line, although the band spent the first month at the Town House in Goldhawk Road, Shepherds Bush, just working on drums.

'*Coming Up* is a very guitar-focussed album,' says Richard, 'so we spent many weeks at Westside, Mayfair, and Master Rock working on the sounds and parts. Despite the separatism back then, there wasn't any separatism with recording, so most members of the band (and various people around the band) would be there when I was recording guitars, and I welcomed that. We were a gang at that point; we were creating a make-or-break follow-up to a fractured second album that almost destroyed Suede...it felt like safety in numbers. I had no problem with people chipping in with ideas or opinions about what I was doing. We all had the same goal.

'It was 1995 and the early days of Pro Tools, so there would inevitably be moments where the computer crashed, and we'd take those opportunities to run upstairs and have a quick game of Wipeout on the studio's PlayStation while the problem was being fixed. Even that felt like a team-building exercise!'

* * *

The songs for *Coming Up* were mostly written apart, then passed about on cassettes. No doubt this songwriting process strikes most modern observers as being a quaint though crude way of conducting mutually inclusive musical activities. And, if you remember, there was a bit of a cassette thing going on with *Dog Man Star*, which may have got us here in the first place. However, I think this is just the way everything worked at the time—and nowadays, of course, the presence of the internet means you don't need the actual real live presence of any of your other band cohorts at all. When it came to recording, the band played through a song with the aim of getting a decent drum take. Then the bass and guitars and keyboards would be recorded separately. That was the studio pattern, although everyone would make suggestions, generally with each member looking after their own corner of a song.

Neil tells me that, being a keyboard player, he would often add his parts towards the end of a given recording, to provide some glue to a track. This meant he was pretty much left to his own devices, or worked more closely with Ed, who, as a keyboard player himself, would understand Neil's intentions and make suggestions. Mat and Simon would have to work together, and the guitars and vocals would have to weave around each other, so Neil's remit was to provide whatever was missing from a track. As *Coming Up* was the first record he had made, he notes, 'The learning curve was pretty steep. Everything was new to me. The best thing to do was to be there as much as I could and try to absorb what was happening, see what every knob and button on every bit of gear did, where you put microphones, what Ed and [mix engineer] Dave Bascombe did to sculpt the mix. There was no time to stop Ed and ask about technical stuff.'

As *Coming Up* was one of the earlier albums recorded on computers using the nascent Pro Tools software, there was a good deal of downtime. Computers would crash and stay crashed, unlike today, when a quick reboot will generally right everything. Downstairs at Master Rock there was a pool table, and satellite TV showing *The Simpsons* at teatime, as well as that PlayStation console (a PS1) upstairs, which all helped to pass the time.

Ed explains how the recording process worked. 'Basically, every track started with acoustic guitar, bongos, tambourine, and Brett, so it all started life pretty much the same way that Marc Bolan recorded all of his stuff originally.' *Coming Up*, he adds, was 'like building a skyscraper'. The main task on the first two records had been the mixing process—on a track like 'Animal Lover', there were twelve different guitar parts to choose from—whereas 'this album was the reverse and designed like a building. The basement was the month of drums all played live. We cut every single bar of drums and kept the bar we liked and had a huge chart on the wall. We didn't want to loop things. Then we did tambourine followed by congas and bongos, and finally acoustic guitars and vocals. This formed the template for the record—with a changeable drum sound—and the full take we had on each song meant we could keep bits from some takes and other takes from other bits. It's an incredibly solid record 'cos the foundation was so great. It was also our first experiment with Pro Tools, which was time-consuming but worth it.' Correspondingly, *Coming Up* was, according to Ed, like 'making a movie, where we used a computer as a giant tape-editing machine: we had lots and lots of takes so we could get the ultimate take'.

Mat Osman recalls how Buller was set on making the album as simple as possible. 'He was really keen on using all those devices: the big, repeated end, the handclaps, the straightforward chorus, make it big and obvious.' Latterly, veteran producer-engineer Dave Bascombe was brought in to mix the album alongside Ed; Ed readily admits that the reason the album has a much better sound than the previous two albums is that he had minimal involvement in the mixing process, mixing only two songs himself. In particular, he points out that Bascombe's input on 'Trash' was crucial, as it was his idea to speed up the vocals.[*]

For the sake of argument, I am assured that, as opposed to the previous album, which followed a stringent pattern of Bernard composing music for Brett's lyrics, *Coming Up* was a more collaborative project. 'It was more of a meritocracy,' says Brett. 'If something was good enough, it didn't matter what the source was.' Famously, *Dog Man Star* had been 'written by post', so the writing arrangements for any new record could only be an upgrade on the band's previous lack of musical empathy. Having said that, Richard still remembers songwriting as being a somewhat separatist activity throughout the period between 1994—when he joined—and 1997. 'Someone would come up with an idea on their own, record it, and present it to someone else.'

Perhaps Brett and Richard are talking at cross purposes here—after all, Brett's version of events is informed by an emotively overwrought retrospective of the *DMS* era, whilst Richard has a more innocent view of proceedings—but they both seem to agree that conviviality thrived. '"Filmstar" and "She" were both unusual in that Brett had a starting point for an idea and came to my house

---

[*] Paradoxically, Brett tells me, 'There are things about the production which I still regret—specifically the Varispeeding of the vocals on a few tracks—but when I listen back to the whole thing with twenty-five years' distance, it still crackles with attitude and energy, and Ed has to be credited for that.'

to sing it to me,' says Richard. 'With the majority of the songs, it would be me, or Neil with "Starcrazy" and "Chemistry", or Mat with "Europe", recording a piece of music alone and either putting a cassette in Brett's hand or pushing it through his letterbox. Then you'd just wait for the results.'

Nevertheless, Brett, at the very least, believes they were breaking a lot of new ground. 'The difference between *Coming Up* and *Dog Man Star*,' he says, 'is bigger than the difference between the first two. The way it was written was revolutionary for us: chuck 'em all in a room and see what happens.' And then, with a dismissive nod towards *Dog Man Star* and that 'written by post' reputation, 'a band has to work on more than the level of turning up and rehearsing and going away again. There has to be a telepathy. With Bernard, we worked separately from the rest of the band, which is why huge bits of *DMS* sound like a solo album. This time I didn't want any solo-ism or any individual performances. It felt like a band playing it. You can't fake that.'

Richard recalls that on odd occasions they would make demos together. 'In fact, Mat came to my flat in '95 and recorded a piece of music called "Anything" that resurfaced in 2000 as "Lost In TV". Once the initial song idea had been formed, we'd rehearse it and turn it into a Suede song. That's when it became collaborative. I never wanted to tell anyone in the band what to play, even when the rehearsing of a song pushed it away from my original vision, which happened quite often. I thought it was more important that everyone got to put their own mark on it, and, having heard the stories of what songwriting and recording was like before I joined, I was eager for there to be freedom of expression from everyone. As far as I'm concerned, every initial idea can be improved upon; changing it doesn't automatically mean ruining it. "Together" was a mid-tempo chord sequence at first, but when Simon got hold of it, he put so much energy and creativity into the drums, the idea changed completely.'

What we also know is that Richard in particular worked very closely with Ed on *Coming Up*. 'I think it was a new thing for Suede that I preferred to be in the control room when recording,' he says now, 'as opposed to (more traditionally) in the live room in front of my amp. I prefer to see people's faces as I'm playing, and have direct communication with them, rather than via headphones and a talkback. Ed was very helpful in my learning process of how to record—I had luckily done several studio sessions with him before we started recording the album, so I knew the process by the time we started at the Townhouse in December. I'd sit and play, and he and Gary'—Gary Stout, Suede's engineer—'would experiment with sounds until we created something we were all happy with. Often, Ed would say to me, *We need a riff here*, and I'd fiddle around until I played something that fitted with what he was imagining. Ed was very into Bowie and T. Rex, and he totally got our own obsession with punk and the Sex Pistols, so the album became a strange mixture of all those approaches.'

The philosophy that informed the overall sound of the album meant that 'Young Men', one of the first songs mooted for inclusion, was left off the record. 'We felt it was too dark,' said Ed at the time. 'We wanted something that was poppy, in your face, very immediate and just full of hooks. We have to make people realise that Suede are a big band and should be treated like one. They are a very important part of our national culture, and they should sell lots of records. So, I think we can have a bit of fun with this album, have a load of hits and establish Suede once and for all as major players in the market.'*

Another song that ended up on the *Coming Up* cutting-room floor was the magnificent 'Europe Is Our Playground', which eventually surfaced as the B-side to 'Trash'. 'We were definitely freer with ideas on B-sides,' says Richard. 'Songs like "This Time" and "Sadie" found their identity from the band taking a basic backing track idea from me and rehearsing it until everyone had written their own essential part. And often a song would drastically change after it was recorded and we started playing it live. The best example with this era is the huge difference between the B-side version of "Europe", recorded during the album sessions in '96, and the "Sci-Fi" version, recorded in '97 after a year of touring.'

Of course, the most pertinent fact about 'Europe Is Our Playground' is that the song marked the arrival of Mat Osman as a songwriter, after 'Sombre Bongos', a chord sequence he'd messed around with on an old electric piano, was re-recorded to reflect its extravagant transformation when performed live. 'I was thrilled,'

---

* 'Young Men' would eventually end up as the B-side to 'Beautiful Ones', the second single to be lifted from the album.

said Mat at the time. 'I couldn't even talk about it. There's always been really good songwriters in Suede who just do it like making a cup of tea. I'd always felt the competition was too great. I felt like Ringo. And you don't want more than one "Octopus's Garden" on the album.' Unfortunately, regardless of the fact that 'Europe Is Our Playground' is no 'Octopus's Garden', it fell victim to the *ten hits* rule. 'I thought it was a really cool track,' says Saul. 'I loved the icy Germanic vibe, which gave me an insight into the future of the band, but I managed to persuade Brett that it didn't suit the album. Brett agreed in the end, or at least we agreed that it didn't sound like a hit! In retrospect, maybe it should have been on *Head Music*.'

That's as maybe, but more importantly, it should be noted that the song had more in common with the band's previous album, and that was just not on. Or, as Saul put it more bluntly at the time, 'There was never any intention to repeat *Dog Man Star*. This is not the same Suede, remember. This is a different band entirely.'

SIDE A ...

5

LET'S DANCE

"Imagine, if you will, a government-
endorsed break-in—or one more likely
financed by the likes of Blur or Oasis—at
the band's studio, and the frantically illicit
rummaging in the dark that produced just
the one item: a cassette with the word
Pisspot scrawled across its spine."

'It's about believing in the romance of the everyday. I really wanted to make a straight-up pop record. We were listening to a lot of 60s pop at the time and were very much inspired by the classic three-and-a-half-minute singles.'

If the obstinate and, dare I say it, *pig-headed* 'We Are The Pigs' had been released as the first single off *Dog Man Star* as a kind of *fuck you* to anyone who thought Suede were namby-pamby southerners, then the first single to advertise *Coming Up*'s wares had to be more . . . savvy. Indeed, if Suede's last three singles chart entries were anything to go by—'We Are The Pigs' and 'The Wild Ones' had both reached the no.18 spot, whilst 'New Generation' peaked at no.21—then the jury was out on whether Suede would ever be able to emulate the success of their first few releases. Or, as someone much crueller than me might have put it: *They'd never be as successful again without Bernard being in the band.*

Enter 'Trash', the most Suede-like Suede song of all time.

'Trash' was like 'a trailer for the album', says Brett, and, for me, outsider pop writ large and just the kind of unapologetic blast of pure joy that Suede fans could cling to—whilst clinging to each other. The opening lyrical salvo—'*Oh maybe, maybe it's the clothes we wear / The tasteless bracelets and the dye in our hair / Maybe it's the kookiness*'—could not have been more cutely targeted at anyone who'd ever had a soft spot for Suede if it had tried—which, ahem, it surely hadn't. And when the chorus arrives—actually, that's a lie, the entire beautiful spectacle is a fucking chorus—you are in

76

no doubt that the *'lovers on the streets'* are, well, *us*! We can't help being who we are, 'Trash' tells us, so let's just celebrate the fact: it's in *everything* we do, after all. It's clever stuff and no more or less than an anthem for the alienated and disaffected. And, in case you are wondering, that's you and me, that is.

In 2013, Brett suggested as much when he revealed, 'It's a song that's kind of about being in the band and, by extension, it's a song about the fans and the whole kind of ethos of being a Suede…person. I actually wrote it about the band Suede, but it's a celebration of the fans as well. And it was a kind of a song written about us, as a gang, it was written about the values we stood for. And even though it sounds like a love song, it was actually about the idea of the identity of the band, and what they stood for.'

In other words, it's the quintessential Suede song.

Neil agrees that, lyrically, the song is a reflection of the band being a gang. 'We had our little manor in Ladbroke Grove, our little dress code, and "Trash" was our signature song for 1996. But it stretched beyond the five of us and our world and acted as a call-to-arms for like-minded people everywhere. That's the power of songwriting when it works: sometimes with a fair wind you can convey a feeling and idea in three minutes that finds disparate people and makes of them a collective who feel the same way, all in the time it takes to hear it on the radio. "Trash" was very much one of those songs for us.'

Twenty-five years after the song was written, Brett hasn't changed his mind about what it means to him. 'It's still a very

77

special song for me,' he says now. 'I wrote it as a kind of band theme song, something that detailed the burgeoning gang mentality that we as a group were feeling.' More importantly, he maintains that 'the song features sentiments that couldn't possibly have been written during—say—the fraught and fractured *Dog Man Star* sessions. It's one of those songs which can be played in very different ways. Of course, when hammered out live on electric guitars, it has a rabble-rousing quality, but there's also a poetry and soulfulness to the song which only comes across if you deliver it more delicately.' Either way, it's a song he's very proud of—an anthem for Suede and, by extension, for Suede fans, a statement of identity. 'I'd grown up in the midst of late-70s tribal pop culture,' he tells me, 'so the identity and the world of the bands I was into was so important to me. I always wanted Suede to be more than just some people that made music. I wanted it to be a hill that people were willing to die on.'

In his book *The Last Party*, John Harris describes 'Trash' as 'a knowing, romantic clarion call to those who saw their experiences reflected in the group's music—the occupants of "nowhere towns" and "nothing places" and "lovers on the streets".' One could hardly disagree, although the key word here is *knowing*: 'Trash' very much *knows* what it is doing—preaching to the converted, perhaps, but doing it with such style and grace that you couldn't help loving it all the more. If you had to sum it up in one word, that word would be *incorrigible*. Or as Dick Emery might have put it—now there's one for the teenagers—'*Ooh, you are awful—but I like you!*'

78

Happily, the critics were in agreement—they all had a meeting—with *Melody Maker* awarding Suede their umpteenth 'Single Of The Week' accolade and hailing the record as 'bitterly sweet, a love song for strangers; fast, in every sense of the word', while the *NME*'s Ted Kessler went even further, suggesting 'the scaremongers were wrong. Brett Anderson is the creative force behind Suede. Here's the proof: this week sees the release of their first post-Bernard Butler single and nobody can really admit that they thought it would sound half as good as it does.' The *Telegraph* was similarly enamoured, calling it an 'instant, flawless, three-minute essence-of-pop, as irresistible as "Satisfaction" or "Ride A White Swan".'

Shit, they noticed the T. Rex thing, I thought at the time, but I swooned nonetheless, almost as if I'd written the fucking thing myself. Much later, the *Guardian*'s Ben Hewitt would roll up his sleeves and gasp, before downing tools for the day: 'A ditty for the downtrodden, a paean for the put-upon, and an anthem for anyone seeking romance in the most humdrum nooks and crannies, it's a view of drab suburban life blitzed into Technicolor excitement, with pistol-shot drums and a squealing, screaming guitar line. Above all else, though, it's Suede's love letter to Suede, a celebration of their knack for finding glamour in squalid surroundings. Anderson's manifesto for all the misfits and lost souls trapped in satellite town hell: forget the jerks and their jeers because you're more beautiful than they could ever be.' Here, if you cock your ears and listen carefully, you will hear me whispering, 'No further questions, your honour.'

HERE THEY COME . . .

Musically, 'it's a Motown thing', said Mat at the time, and 'a lot of the tracks on the album have really rigid grooves, a real clockwork sound.' Perhaps, he's right, although I've always hated Motown—apart from 'Motown Junk' by the Manic Street Preachers, does that count?—and the first time I heard it, it reminded me of the first time I heard 'Modern Love', the opening track off Bowie's *Let's Dance*: it was a mite unexpected, and perhaps too fast for its own good, but it got my attention with bells on. *Oh, and another thing*, I thought at the time, *how the hell did you pull off something like that when no one was looking?*

The original working title for 'Trash' was 'Pisspot'. 'Richard was very keen on coming up with offensive working titles just so he could ask the engineer, Can you get up the drum tracks for "Pisspot"?' revealed Mat in the September 1996 issue of *Select* magazine. Latterly, Brett has claimed responsibility for the 'Pisspot' moniker, just so they didn't have to keep referring to 'Trash' as *that new song with the guitar bit on it*, although he readily admits that he never expected any working titles to go further than the band.

Having said that, at the time, I can recall Blur naming their recently purchased greyhound *Far Canal* just so they could crack up laughing as the race commentator followed the dog's progress at breakneck speed over the Tannoy—do try this at home—whenever it competed at Walthamstow Greyhound Stadium, so Suede's wordplay juvenilia was not without precedent in the wider rock community. However, I can't help thinking that the band's tendency to mis-moniker their songs at this stage of proceedings was simply a ruse intended to ensure all interested parties were put off thinking the record would be an instant chart success. Perhaps several members of the band would disagree, but imagine, if you will, a government-endorsed break-in—or one more likely financed by the likes of Blur or Oasis—at the band's studio, and the frantically illicit rummaging in the dark that produced just the one item: a cassette with the word *Pisspot* scrawled across its spine.

'Wotcha got?' would be the initial enquiry.

'Nuffink,' would be the reply.

And they'd be gone, leaving us all to ruminate on whether the suspected intruders emanated from north or south of the Watford Gap.

Of course, the theory touched on above is hardly countered by the news that 'Trash' was very late to the party indeed. 'After months of writing, we still didn't feel like we had the definitive single to start the record,' says Brett. '"Trash" was a strange song. It went through so many changes that it became a bit of a Trigger's Broom—something that is unrecognisable from its starting point. There's a popular trope amongst the public that songwriting is a single moment of enlightenment and magic, but in reality, of course, it's far less romantic a process. "Trash" was particularly hard to get right—sometimes the good ones are, sometimes they're not, there's no one formula. But, one day, Richard came up with a beautiful, elegant chord sequence which inspired me to write an anthem to the outsider. "Trash" is possibly my proudest moment ever as a lyricist. Still documenting the outsider, but this time with a smile on his face.'

The '*litter on the breeze*' lyric in particular is, according to Ed Buller, 'Suede in a nutshell. Getting "Trash",' he says now, 'was like getting the last digit in a phone number.' 'Trash' was also the only potential *Coming Up* tune that Saul Galpern didn't hear as an early demo, although it ended up as the song that would 'glue the album together'.

'We had an emergency meeting one Sunday round at Nude,' says Saul, 'and it's probably true to say that I gave Brett a bit of a grilling. We had spent a lot of money, and I had given the band carte blanche to work in any studio they'd wanted—'cos I believed in them, and it was important that Ed had the right space to make the best record ever—but I just didn't think we had that first single, so I had to lay it on the line. Brett was none too pleased, and I felt guilty about it immediately afterwards—but it did the trick.'

Nothing, however, had prepared Saul for the song he heard once he was summoned to the Townhouse Studios towards the end of the recording sessions. 'I knew something was going on,' he says now. 'It was like they were playing games with me. They obviously knew they were on to something—there was a confidence in the air that indicated they had written a banger—but it was like they kept it secret from me to the last minute.' Naturally, the plot thickens, but Saul knew immediately he had a smash hit on his hands. 'It wasn't finished by any means,' he says, 'but the chorus got me really excited, and I remember feeling goosebumps. This was the anthem I was looking for.' Funnily enough, the discovery of such an 'anthem' sent Saul into a tailspin: 'Dodgy were all over the radio at the time with "Good Enough". And I told the sales team that the record had to go in higher than fucking Dodgy.'

I know, *Dodgy!* But such was the paranoia accompanying the band at the time.

In the intervening years since its release, *Coming Up* has spawned various reissues and special editions, and these have included early versions of 'Trash', including a four-track demo of 'Pisspot', with alternate lyrics about fishes and colour TVs. Richard now tells me he has found just about every single tape of all the different versions of 'Trash' during its evolution, including the Dictaphone tape of his very first idea in October 1995. Somewhat revealingly, he says, 'It bears zero resemblance to the finished song! It really was just another piece until I wrote a new chorus for it, which people thought was a winner. But the verse was too jagged and odd, so we played around with another verse idea that was okay, nothing that special . . . then Brett almost spontaneously wrote the perfect verse for it in the studio in about February 1996, and then it was finished.' Correspondingly, Brett remembers not liking the old verse to the song, writing some chords for a new verse, and it being such a 'weird' song to begin with that he is glad it became 'a different song entirely'.

'I had a fiddly arpeggiated guitar line for the verse at first,' says Richard, 'but when Mat and Simon put that simple, driving rhythm track down, I knew I had to attack it a bit more, so I put a Stones-y rhythmic part down that worked better. But the music didn't get its icing until Ed put that Moog line down on the verses, then suddenly it was the euphoric, romantic, *Coming Up*-shaped piece that it needed to be. Brett found the lyric and it became the obvious choice for first single. I was very pleased with how it turned out after such a long journey, it shows its worth persevering with an idea and it always feels like our ultimate statement when we play it at gigs.'

In 2021, Ed Buller told *Guitar* magazine's Andy Price that he could remember Brett picking up an acoustic guitar one afternoon at Westside and playing through a new verse idea built around a C–Em–F–D–G sequence. 'We changed one chord at the end and it was done. "Trash" just felt ordained when they came up with the verse.' Naturally, there were further challenges—after all, the song was set to be Richard's inaugural spotlight solo—but 'the tone was Ampulator and DI'd fuzz,' Ed told Price. 'We were at Master Rock, who had the world's first Focusrite console, they had great transformers and preamps, so we just overloaded it. It's the same process that made the guitar sound for *Revolution* back in 1968—overloading the preamp and essentially turning the mixing desk into a massive fuzz box.'

Neil is adamant that the chorus of 'Trash' is so triumphant that most of the work around it was finding a verse that fitted, that set the chords up nicely, and that was on a par with the chorus. 'Like a lot of songwriting,' he says, 'you don't know how to fix it until, through trial and error, you come across something that works.

Everything is wrong until it's right. Brett came up with the verse almost off-the-cuff in the studio. Its meandering melody set the chorus up perfectly and took the song to the next level.'

Another important addition to the verse was the recurrent synthesizer line reminiscent of the guitar motif played by Robert Fripp on David Bowie's 'Heroes'. 'It's hard to conceive of now,' says Neil, 'but "Heroes" wasn't a hit record and David Bowie's stock was comparatively low when Suede came along: he'd spent a decade being an out-and-out pop star and then moved on to Tin Machine. As a musical reference at a time when bands were referencing The Beatles and The Kinks, it was rather niche by comparison.'*

These days, Brett regards 'Trash' as 'an incredibly important song that defined my tribe, something I was looking for my whole life. When I was a child I never quite fitted in and my family never quite fitted in, and I think I was looking for that.' In 2003, he told the *Independent*, 'I don't try and consciously create a blueprint for people's lives. But I was a lot more conscious back then of speaking to an alternative community of people which I was sure populated the world. I always think of the Suede community as being this international society of suburbanites and loners.'

Mat Osman recognised this Suede community as a 'mongrel nation which only exists at the gigs and on the net, who live in these forgotten half-arsed pathetic towns.' Well, somehow, this

---

* 'Heroes' only reached no.24 in the UK charts and no.126 in the USA when it was first released.

'mongrel nation' propelled 'Trash', when it was released on July 29, 1996, to no.3 in the UK, its sales of sixty thousand copies dwarfing Suede's other no.3 hit, 'Stay Together'—a record that had appeared as far back as Valentine's Day, 1994. In subsequent weeks, the single would go on to be no.1 in Finland and become a smash hit in Denmark, Iceland, and Sweden, leading Brett to speculate whether this was 'because they're all depressed sex maniacs, or something'. I am constantly assured that they're not, but it's good to know they were loved, nonetheless.

Eighteen years after its release, US music magazine *Paste* placed 'Trash' at no.14 in a list of the 50 Best Britpop Songs, while the *NME* placed it at no.9 in its public poll of the 50 Greatest Britpop Songs Ever. 'Trash', it said, 'made being a glam weirdo seem like the most appealing thing in the world.'

Oh, and Dodgy's 'Good Enough'? It went to no.4.

Just ten hits?

One down, nine to go.

6

CHILDREN OF THE REVOLUTION

"On 'Filmstar', Brett's vocal delivery has never sounded more sarf London/soft cockney as he barks indifferently about *cla-rss* and *living it fast*, harking back to the line about the *lovely little number* on 'Moving' from their debut album, three years earlier. For a moment, you expect him to yell, 'You're only supposed to blow the bloody doors off!'**"**

'*When everyone else was running around saying Suede
can't carry on, I was sitting there plotting the next album,
and I knew it was going to be good. I just let everyone
else panic around me. It's something that I look at from a
distance and sort of smile at and think, Wait and see.*'

After the manic aural delights of 'Trash', you could be forgiven
for wanting some respite. If so, you've come to the wrong place,
as 'Filmstar', which follows, kicks off with a Pistols-type guitar
riff that menacingly follows Brett around the room for the entire
duration of the song.

The Pistols guitar thing is, of course, a fairly obvious
observation—both Brett and Richard remain massive fans of the Sex
Pistols and Steve Jones's guitar sound on *Never Mind The Bollocks*—
but the T. Rex influence here is perhaps even more apparent. Ed
Buller suggests that the Holy Grail in pop music is a kind of
distorted guitar that is aggressive but not X-rated—presumably like
a movie release that is attempting to sneak into the arena of public
acceptance without being lumbered with an X certificate. 'Hendrix
was too far,' says Ed, 'but T. Rex was all right. So you are trying
to get the guitar sound to the edge of acceptability. *Never Mind
The Bollocks* has an amazing guitar sound, but it's not X-rated. The
record only becomes X-rated if you add Johnny Rotten to the mix.
If you think about it, the first two Suede albums are Bowie, and
Coming Up is more T. Rex and the Pistols.'

Essentially a song about a certain kind of English actor—think

Terence Stamp or Alan Bates—who makes what he does look easy, the vagaries of 'Filmstar' make it difficult to work out whether Brett approves or disapproves of the character he is singing about. My view on such matters is backed up by Brett, who lets on that he likes that the lyric is so deliberately *blank*. 'I suppose I was slightly playing with subverting my own reputation as a veiled, poetic sort of writer,' he tells me. 'So I enjoyed writing a song that only had one layer of meaning. I guess the exact reference is fairly irrelevant, but people like that sort of thing, so if pushed I'd say it was inspired by Alan Bates. At the time, I was obsessed with one of his films from the late 70s called *The Shout*.'

On 'Filmstar', Brett's vocal delivery has never sounded more sarf London/soft cockney as he barks indifferently about '*cla-rss*' and '*living it fast*', harking back to the line about the '*lovely little number*' on 'Moving' from their debut album, three years earlier. For a moment, you expect him to yell, 'You're only supposed to blow the bloody doors off!' Instead, he croons, '*What to believe in, it's impossible to say*' amidst '*changing names*' and '*washing brains*' shenanigans, thus perfectly capturing the heart of the matter: our celluloid heroes are pretending to be something they're not, and we're all in on the game.

Oh, and whilst we are on the subject of Brett's vocal affectations—and particularly those of the identifiably London variety—you should probably be made aware that when Suede were in the studio recording 'The Drowners', Nude boss Saul Galpern asked producer Ed Buller if he could do anything about Brett's cockney accent, and—with particular reference to lines like '*You're taking me ov-ah*'—whether he could get Brett 'to dial this back a bit'.

It's odd that I think of 'Moving' when I think of 'Filmstar', as Neil also seems to think the two songs have something in common. Of course, he has a much more sophisticated way of comparing the two songs, citing their schizophrenic change of mood from verse to chorus. Indeed, it's here that he starts to put me in my place by coming over 'as a musicologist for a bit, that shift from brutal/visceral to sweeping/contemplative, a musical switch from chromatic in the verse to diatonic in the chorus (with a common Suede-like return to chromaticism at the end of the chorus), along with the lyrical move from impressionistic to philosophical, is emblematic of the sweep that the band can cover, packed into a catchy three-minute pop song. Like "The Drowners", you can't dance to it, but it's still anthemic. "Filmstar" has a punk vibe in the sense of the Pistols' take on punk. The Sex Pistols tended to write different kinds of songs from the amphetamine rush of "Spiral Scratch" or "New Rose": their stuff is slower, grander. Ed likes the Pistols, but not much other punk rock. I think this is down to an innate poppiness in the Pistols: Glen Matlock was famously inspired to write the music to "Pretty Vacant" after hearing "SOS" by ABBA. So, yes, that punk edge is/was a constant, conscious influence on Suede. Simon was a punk growing up, and Brett and Richard both love it. I was steeped in it too: I first heard it aged three or four when my brother used to play the Pistols, the Clash, Stiff Little Fingers, and the Angelic Upstarts at home.'

90

'Filmstar' was one of the songs written before Neil arrived on the scene, and he readily admits that he didn't add much beyond some keyboard sounds in the instrumental verse. He did however play some tom fills on the drums when he was in the studio one day when Simon wasn't around—even though Simon was only a ten-minute car ride away—a fact that may be news to Suede's much-loved stickman to this day.

Brett tells me that 'Filmstar' was 'the first great song that Richard and I wrote for *Coming Up*. Contrary to the whole laboured way in which we wrote "Trash", "Filmstar"'s birth was actually incredibly simple and instinctive. I remember waking up one morning with the verse melody and lyric looping in my head and rushing round to Richard's flat and tapping out the crude rhythm on my knees and him threading the riff around my vocal part. After a couple of hours, the song was written, and essentially it didn't change much up until the moment we recorded it.'

Richard confirms Brett's recollection of bashing out rhythms on knees. He also agrees with Neil that 'the song did end up as a kind of punk/Pistols thing, but it didn't begin like that. Brett had an idea for a lyric and a melody. Brett came over to my flat to sing it. I wrote a simple descending power chord for the verses, which was quite unlike me as I usually prefer to do more complicated things on the guitar. As I recall, the resulting home demo was slow and lumbering; it didn't really find its identity until Simon turned the rhythm into a primal, pounding drumbeat and we recorded a short, simple demo of it at the Church that everyone was excited about.'

91

Ed Buller maintains that 'Filmstar' originally had just one verse; Brett had to be persuaded to add more. 'We started off with a tempo very like "Children Of The Revolution",' he says, 'but it was too dirge-like, so it changed. One of the things we wanted to do on this LP was to have the whole band playing on the tracks. This time, for, instance, Brett played all the extra percussion.'

'When Brett had something to play me,' says Saul Galpern, 'he usually would just turn up at the office unannounced and walk straight up the stairs into my office—even if I was on the phone or in a meeting. Nothing could wait, and that's what happened with "Filmstar". I remember being very excited about it—though I thought it was more *rock* glam than *punk* glam—but I could hear it being an A-list track for the album. I suppose what I had to get used to was the simplistic chords Richard was playing: really good riffs, but less complicated chords than Bernard.'

Elsewhere on 'Filmstar', there are handclaps by Boy George and his band—they were recording in the next room at Mayfair Studios at the time—and Brett's reference to *'driving in a car, it looks so easy'* is surely par for the course. Famously, Brett couldn't drive until comparatively recently—'He's more obsessed with cars than anyone I know,' complained Mat Osman back in the day, 'and he never got to borrow the older brother's Capri when he was seventeen and get it out of his system'—and certainly, *Coming Up* coincided with the bulk of Brett's non-driving activities. Two further tracks on the album feature *'petrol fumes'* ('Picnic By The Motorway') and the excitable phrase *'high on diesel and gasoline'*

('Beautiful Ones'), but it's not as if we haven't been here before: 'Bentswood Boys' boasted, '*When you're high on diesel, nightly*' back in 1994; '*He hired a car for you*' turned up in 'The Next Life'; and '*He crashed the car and left us here / With dreams of gasoline drying our eyes*' surfaced on 'Daddy's Speeding'. Indeed, if you wanted to be churlish about such things, you could say that Brett often felt the need to abandon the concept of privately owned vehicles altogether: on 'Another No One', he sings, '*Outside is just a taxi ride to drive away / So she packs her bag, calls a cab and the world smiles.*' And who can forget his sublime protestations on 'The Asphalt World', '*Sometimes we ride in a taxi to the ends of the city*'?

Richard remembers Ed seeing something 'much more poppy in "Filmstar", so it evolved further when we recorded it for the album, gaining a middle eight and extended outro.' 'Filmstar' was now beginning to sound like a single, but 'the guitar sounds are all Ed,' adds Richard. 'He definitely used a few signature sounds on the song. I remember layering up the same parts over and over again as he wanted the riffs to sound huge.'

Naturally, Richard's reference to huge riffs reminds me that *Coming Up* features more than its fair share of songs that arrive from the off, sporting enormous guitar riffs that you wouldn't normally associate with a band like Suede, or an album generally regarded as something of a pop record. 'Trash' and 'Beautiful Ones' and 'Starcrazy' in particular all shoot out of the blocks, guitar-wise, and 'Filmstar' is no exception.

Richard agrees. 'Yes,' he says, 'in-your-face intros with big riffs was a definite rule for *Coming Up*. We didn't want to have any slow burner songs on the album, even though "Picnic" and "Saturday Night" are pretty meandering at the start. It's strange when we play it live because, as per "The Drowners", even though audiences are into it, it's exactly the wrong tempo to jump up and down to.'

For Saul Galpern, 'Filmstar' was 'the first one to me that I thought was really good,' although at that point he wasn't sure if it was a single. Having said as much, Brett can only remember feeling relief once they'd finished the song. 'It felt like finally I could see an identity for the album and a way forward for the band,' he says. 'You can really hear Richard's post-punk influences on this track—he brought a brilliant gnarliness to it which I could never have achieved on my own.'

That *gnarliness* paid dividends when, on August 11, 1997, almost a year after 'Trash', ahem, trashed the charts, 'Filmstar' became the fifth single lifted off *Coming Up* to reach the Top 10. The success of the song as a single in its own right, and so long after the album's release, ensured that *Coming Up* became something of a phenomenon. Moreover, the album had achieved another landmark: aside from Take That, Suede were now the only band that had achieved five Top 10 singles off the same album.

At the risk of sounding foolish, the success of 'Filmstar' also meant that I started to think about the impossibility of it all, by which I mean to say, was Brett's original conception of *Coming Up* as 'ten hits' about to bear fruit? *Five hits. Five more to go?*

7

AS LOVELY AS THE CLOUDS...

❝I listened to 'Lazy' three times this morning before getting out of bed. I hated it, then I listened to it again and hated it even more. There's a good chance that, when I get home tonight, I'll listen to the song again, and I'm pretty sure I'll hate it all over again.❞

'It's about two people getting wasted and then looking out the window the next morning, watching people drive to Sainsbury's.'

I listened to 'Lazy' three times this morning before getting out of bed. I hated it, then I listened to it again and hated it even more. There's a good chance that, when I get home tonight, I'll listen to the song again, and I'm pretty sure I'll hate it all over again. In fact, I can't think of a time when I've listened to this song and not hated it. Musically it may be 'the simplest thing we've done'—thank you, Mat Osman!—but it's like a nursery rhyme, and I am not a child. Thank you, Suede, for treating me like a child.

'Lazy' is short, infuriating, and immensely entertaining, but it was a pretty old song when it arrived at the doors of the *Coming Up* studios. 'I remember Brett playing it at a soundcheck years ago,' said Mat at the time of the album's release, and it was such a personal favourite of Brett's that he took a rough mix from the studio and played it on an endless loop at top volume in his new flat in Chesterton Road in Ladbroke Grove.

Ed Buller also remembers 'Lazy' as an old song and even something that Bernard may have rejected in less sunnier climes. Indeed, Ed now suggests that 'Lazy' only got a look in during the *Coming Up* selection process as several other contenders—including perhaps 'Young Men' and 'Money'—just weren't up to the job. He goes on to dismiss 'Lazy' and the album's closing track, 'Saturday Night', as 'meat-and-two-veg songs that don't destroy the record but don't add much to it either', as well as his two least favourite songs on the record.

Having damned 'Lazy' with the faintest of praise, Ed's further pronouncements on the song prove to be most illuminating. The song starts with some gently oscillating guitar shenanigans that seem to be trapped in an echo chamber but, as Ed explains, the guitar sound on 'Lazy' is a perfect example of the kind of synthetic, electronic, and processed sound they had been looking for from the off. Ed, Brett, and Richard had been talking about the guitar sounds on *Slider* and *Tanx* and how they could make them more twenty-first century—or *a bit trippier and weirder.* 'We used a lot of boxes,' Ed says now, 'and I borrowed a box from [fellow producer] Flood called an ADA Ampulator, a nineteen-inch single-unit rack miniature tube power amp and speaker cab emulator, which is basically the front end of an amplifier. The classic, electronic-y, guitar sound we got is meant to sound brittle and processed.'*

After that initial brittle, processed, electronic-y guitar refrain, another casually administered pluck of a single, low guitar string

---

* Flood's real name is Mark Ellis, but aside from the fact that he has produced some of the most successful and influential bands in the world, including the likes of U2, Smashing Pumpkins, Nine Inch Nails, New Order, and Depeche Mode, my favourite—possibly apocryphal—story about him relates to how he became known as Flood in the first place. Working as one of two young studio runners at Morgan Studios, whilst The Cure were in residence, he managed to provide numerous cups of tea for the assembled musicians and staff whilst his erstwhile running companion remained largely unavailable; you can guess which one got nicknamed Flood, and perhaps even which one ended up with the moniker *Drought.*

signals the beginning of one of the most effortlessly complacent verse-chorus-verse-chorus machines you're likely to encounter this side of a pop songwriting masterclass. Having realised as much, the first thing you notice are the squeaky vocals, a result of speeding up the mix to accommodate the fact that Brett was smoking too much and couldn't get the words out. 'Brett denies that his smoking affected the recording,' says Ed, 'but Dave Bascombe did a fantastic job on this mix in particular.' Ed also suggests that the 'wrong' chord that leads into the chorus is a signature Suede trick to add to the drama. Presumably that casually administered pluck I just referred to is a case in point, but it's only when Ed moves on to talk about the contrasts between Richard and Bernard's approach to playing guitar that I start to understand the fundamental differences between *Coming Up* and the first two Suede albums.

'Bernard is a virtuoso,' he explains, 'but he gets bored of playing the same thing twice, so you rarely get the same thing twice! Richard is more disciplined and spends all his time getting the part right. That meant we could spend a lot more time working on the sound. We spent three days on the guitars for "Lazy"'—I get the impression that every song on *Coming Up* called for such attention to detail—'and the record wouldn't have been as disciplined or structured if Bernard had been on it. The crucial songs on the first album were "Pantomime Horse" and "Animal Nitrate", as they showed the breadth of the band's repertoire. *Dog Man Star* was ambitious and driven by Bernard's musicality, and if he'd had his way it wouldn't have featured so many vocals. *Coming Up* had to be more streamlined and was designed to be a condensed version of the band at their poppiest.'

Which is presumably where Richard stepped in.

Neil says he did very little on 'Lazy' beyond a bit of chorus Mellotron and some backing vocals, notably the high octave on the first line of each chorus. 'Like "Beautiful Ones",' he suggests, 'it all came together when we nailed the verse guitar sound. I remember we aimed for a Beatles-y guitar tone. We put "I Feel Fine"—renowned for its opening feedback noise—on the studio speakers to see what a classic, jangly guitar sound sounded like, and it was, by modern standards, very polite with very little chime or sustain. That's why chasing a retro sound or feel got you nowhere, as music moves on so quicky. What was cutting-edge in 1964 sounded pretty blunt over thirty years later. You could probably say the same about guitars on "Lazy" now. It was a song of its time—it had an indie sensibility and a classic 60s feel as well as sounding 90s—and although it was a single, we tend not to play it live beyond *Coming Up* gigs or the odd festival outing these days.'

Richard lets on that when Brett presented the first version of 'Lazy' to the rest of the band in June 1995, 'it was a very light, woozy acoustic demo that had "I'm Only Sleeping" vibes to it. We knew we had to toughen it up, so it became faster and more riff heavy to fit in with the sonic template of the album.' Mat agrees that 'Lazy' was one of the songs that needed guitar, 'otherwise

99

it was gonna get beaten up by the others', but it was only when Richard wrote the wiry guitar part for the choruses, which only later became the intro—the song had originally started with drums—that people started to get excited about it and it started to 'bounce as a song'. The 'bounce' thing is interesting, as when the band play the song live, it always inspires their frenzied crowd to bounce up and down, united in a gentle pogo that doesn't quite fit the song or the surroundings.

Richard reveals that 'Lazy' developed into something more tangible 'when Mat nailed a bass line and Neil added Mellotrons and very high backing vocals, which gave it a sparkle. It was part of the family and another potential single. I think you can tell it's an older song because it has a kind of innocence and naivety to it, which survived despite its toughening up.'

Brett tells me that 'Lazy' is 'very much a vignette of mine and Alan's marginal life at the time'—Alan is Alan Fisher, Brett's long-term best friend and erstwhile flatmate, who occasionally held down a job working in a chip shop in Oxted—'two frazzled, fractured souls trying to negotiate the bleak mornings-after. It's the same song as "Trash", really, just two people off their faces one morning and they look out their window and there's this procession of people going by. Along with "By The Sea", it was one of a brace of songs I wrote on my own while Bernard was still in the band. To be honest, it's not my favourite song on *Coming Up* and would hardly be worth including if it wasn't for Richard's excellent Roger McGuinn-style guitar part.'

Lyrically, the song is as bonkers as ever. The original first line was '*As lovely as the clouds on my ceiling*', which is explained away by the fact that when Brett was a kid, his mum painted his bedroom ceiling with blue and white clouds and he hung his model Airfix planes there with 'little threads of cotton and drawing pins'. It's all delightfully drole, but '*Boys and girls and their mums and their words*' leaves us in no doubt how our casual interlocuters view proceedings: dismissively, and as the perfect foil to their drug-addled, work-shy pursuits.

I'm being disingenuous, of course, but 'Lazy' does feature several other charming turns of phrase: '*Barking mad kids lonely dads*' and '*Uncle Teds and their legendary vests*' immediately spring to mind. The song is 'about two people getting wasted and then looking out the window the next morning, watching people drive to Sainsbury's,' says Brett, and you can almost smell the bread counter as he hollers a reminder about '*things to be done*'. The sentiment is dripping with a kind of mocking ennui that implies that anyone outside Brett and Alan's world of drug-induced paranoia is an imposter of the highest order. Don't they know it's just gone 7am?

Released as a single on April 7, 1997, 'Lazy' became the fourth track off *Coming Up* to reach the UK Top 10, peaking at no.9. The B-sides on CD1—the Anderson/Oakes composition 'These Are The Sad Songs' and the full band effort 'Feel'—were written to order and produced by acclaimed engineer/producer/mixer Bruce Lampkov; interestingly, CD2 featured 'Digging A Hole', a song written and performed solo by Neil Codling.

Of course, having started off by giving the song such a hard time, I am finally forced to leap to its defence: 'Lazy' is the perfect companion piece to 'Saturday Night'—a song that turns up much later on the record. Indeed, if 'Saturday Night' is the song you play when you're getting ready to go out, 'Lazy' is the song you play—on a continuous loop—in the morning. After you've stayed up all night. But it's also much more than that: the song is so effortlessly beguiling that it feels like something you've had knocking around the house for years. Or, dare I say it, it stands as empirical evidence that Brett had now started to write songs like this in his sleep.

You can't get lazier than that.

8

URBAN HYMNS

"Suede have so many songs rooted in the seedy glitz of the city—and London in particular—that it comes as something of a shock to find them dreaming of running away.**"**

'There were only a handful of people in the world who still really believed in Suede at the time and five of them were in the band.'

Brett Anderson once claimed that he found it easy to write epic sweeping ballads, and if that's true then he must have found 'By The Sea' a doddle. Written whilst Suede were working on their debut album—this could explain why the song's first line, *'She can walk out anytime'*, is so similar to the opening line to 'So Young'— 'By The Sea' is pure daydream escapism, and features some of my favourite lyrics on the album.

Brett reveals that 'the chord sequence is a bit *my first song*', but that was because he was only just learning the rudiments of the piano at the time. 'For a song that nicks the chords of "Puff The Magic Dragon",' he says, 'it manages to be strangely dignified!' For my part, I have to admit that I'm a bit of a sucker for those *I'm not saying what I really mean* songs—10cc's 'I'm Not In Love' and Jon Waite's '(I Ain't) Missing You' immediately spring to mind— and Brett's switch from third to first person and from a male to female POV only serves to enhance the ensuing melodrama. Of course, Brett's opening announcement is of the *doth protest too much* variety, so it is with a nod and a wink that we accompany him throughout the ensuing melodrama.

Brett says he wrote 'By The Sea' 'in around 1993, at my old upright piano, which sat in the flat in Moorhouse Road in Notting Hill'. The flat was an important place for Brett and somewhere he slowly became someone. 'It's where I wrote my parts to all those early songs,' he says now, 'and its scruffy grandeur somehow fed into the band persona that was forming.'

The song had been hanging around at rehearsals and soundchecks well before Richard arrived on the scene, although the band had started rehearsing it in the summer of '95 with a view to playing it as a new song at some of the festivals. 'It got a basic band structure,' says Richard. 'I took Brett's rudimentary—he won't mind me saying—piano playing and turned it into more of a rolling part. We played it at a couple of summer festivals, including Phoenix.'

'By The Sea' ultimately evolved into one of the most beautiful songs in a catalogue of such things after the band worked on it in the studio. 'Neil took my piano pattern and turned it into something more unusual and Velvet Underground-like,' says Richard. 'Ed added some trippy synths, and the whole song became less traditional and more unique and that made it fit in with the album. I didn't really contribute anything guitar-wise that changed the song, just a fluid lead guitar part in the third verse. It's a piano song, really, and one I always love playing live.'

I had always assumed that 'By The Sea' was one of the few songs shortlisted for inclusion on *Coming Up* that would require keyboards for live outings, and that this was one of the reasons Brett asked Neil to join Suede in the first place. Naturally, Neil disagrees with my assessment, or at least points out that what the song actually needed when performed live was guitar. 'Richard had played piano on it at Suede's Phoenix show, and it had sounded Suedey and full, but once we got it in the studio it needed filling out, arrangement-wise.' He extrapolates further, 'Having me on piano enabled Richard to tease some atmospheric sounds from the guitar at gigs using his EBow (though in the studio a lot of those sounds were made using synths). It also enabled the song to pick up from verse three onwards as Richard dug in on the guitar.'

'By The Sea' marked Neil's first official day in the recording studio with Suede, or at least the first occasion where he was sent off to a live room to provide some keyboards. Ed remembers him initially trying to play the piano part 'like Rachmaninov', which proved inappropriate, since he felt the song needed the kind of 'fist piano' you'd find on the Velvets' 'Waiting For My Man' or a Nico song. Neil confirms that it took a while to get the piano right, as 'Ed had a dislike of singer/songwriter-like piano parts' and wanted him to play the verse part like 'All Tomorrow's Parties'. That didn't quite fit, so the band ended up recording a composite of two simplified piano parts to steer it away from rock ballad territory. 'That was a balancing act' says Neil, 'because we couldn't have it sounding too ballad-y that early on the record.'

At various junctures on the song, Brett makes the male and female protagonist repeat one another—they both talk about starting new lives and not touching the ground—and it's within this charming exchange of shared perspective that the true extent of the song's complicity in the couple's escapist rhetoric is revealed: '*I'm gonna try hard this time*' implies he/she/*they* have failed at least once in ensuring their feet don't '*touch the ground*' when they're trying to flee the city.

'It's a simple escape song that romanticised some sort of other, distant life,' says Brett. 'I think a lot of city-dwellers idealise places like the countryside and the coast, often ignoring the fact that life anywhere is brutal and hard and often depressing. Sometimes though we are lucky enough to stumble upon those moments of magic that make us all want to carry on.'

'This time,' however, things do seem to work out, as Brett reveals they *'sold the car and quit the job'*, leaving Seven Sisters behind *'for a room in a seaside shack'*. 'By The Sea' may be 'a soft, splashy ode to the virtues of simple living and jacking in the smog and murk of the big smoke', but it's hard to fathom whether we really are in the presence of a redemptive plot, or just inhabiting an illusion dreamt up by the song's protagonists. Oh, it's a cornucopia of mischief, all right.

Suede have so many songs rooted in the seedy glitz of the city—and London in particular—that it comes as something of a shock to find them dreaming of running away. Mat Osman admits the song is 'about urban escape, about something we'd probably never do—leave the city and head for the seaside. It's a reversal, really, because when we were growing up, we dreamed of leaving the quiet, nowhere town.' But we have been here before: on 'The Next Life', one of Suede's most dramatic, epic, sweeping ballads—and the song that signs off the band's eponymous debut long player—Brett gently reflects on driving down to Worthing, where we can *'flog ice creams 'til the company's on its knees'*.

'The Next Life' is ostensibly about the death of Brett's mother—

in his first book, *Coal Black Mornings*, he suggests the song's lyrics were written 'as a general meditation on loss', only realising years later they were 'so crushingly obviously about my mother'—but there's surely something else going on here. Some have argued that 'The Next Life' and 'By The Sea' are about suicide—the latter song features 'Byron-esque lovers', says Ed, and its revelation that the singer can walk '*across the sand into the sea into the brine*' could indicate that he will drown himself. But I can't help seeing the two songs as the most recalcitrant of bedfellows, merely cleverly nuanced, absent-minded reflections on what it would be like to get away from it all. By the kiss-off line, they've gotten down there safely enough—and, in my imagination, it's always *down* there. It is Brighton, it is Hastings; heaven forbid, it is Worthing again. But I don't think it indicates any kind of suicide pact.

9

NOWHERE FACES

❝I think it's important to point out that 'She' is also a very weird song. Savagely melodramatic in both execution and delivery, it's only after a couple of listens that you realise the chorus is really just a more manically rearranged version of the verse, and then another couple more before you notice you've been singing along to pretty much the same words throughout the entire three and a half minutes of its existence.**❞**

'I would agree that there's a Suede vocabulary. I do use a lot of the same words and I'd like to have a patent on them.'

'She' is one of six Anderson/Oakes compositions on the record—elsewhere, you'll find two Anderson/Codling co-writes and two Anderson self-penned numbers—but it's the stunning string arrangement by Craig Armstrong that steals the show. Armstrong had recently worked on the song 'Goldeneye', performed by Tina Turner for the 1995 James Bond movie of the same name, and he was the perfect fit for a song that producer Ed Buller always saw as 'very filmic . . . John Barry, 60s movies. In fact, when we were recording it, Richard would break into the theme from the Pink Panther movies.'

Craig recalls Brett liking an arrangement he'd done for Massive Attack two years before *Coming Up* and being happy about that, as he had always been a huge Suede fan. 'They seemed to be like a band you would have loved to have been in,' he says now. 'When a song is as good as "She", the arrangement almost writes itself. I feel the same about films too; when working with Baz Luhrmann there is so much inspiration already in the picture, so it's much easier to write for these incredibly inspiring works.'

Richard tells me that the band wrote 'She' not long after 'Filmstar' and in exactly the same way, Brett singing the melody 'and tapping out a drum part, and me writing the chords and melodic information around that. Brett was into very simple lyrics and vocal melodies at that point, and "She" seemed to nail this perfectly.' It was one of the five or six songs that Ed heard at a first meeting at Brett's house back in late October 1995, and he knew immediately that it needed strings.

As a long-term John Barry fan, Ed's initial conversations with Armstrong centred on the song having a Bond-edge—'You Only Live Twice' and 'Diamonds Are Forever' were reference points— but Ed was acutely aware that Suede had a somewhat chequered past when using string arrangements on previous releases: 'Sleeping Pills', one of the more elaborately conceived tracks on their debut album, features a gorgeous string arrangement envisaged and enabled by Ed's father, John Buller, and the presence of those strings had set the bar high. Subsequently, the strings employed on *Dog Man Star* had proven somewhat problematic and, according to Ed, 'too knowingly self-reverential'.

There's little denying that the addition of strings leaves an indelible mark on 'She'. Indeed, Ed maintains that they provide both 'a shimmer and an evil edge' to the song, and perhaps there's even 'something of *Cabaret* about it.' He attempts to explain this away by suggesting that 'that gender thing' had surfaced again within the lyrics of the song, but when I tell him that every time I see Brett perform 'She' live he looks like he feels sexy, he laughs. 'Brett is always sexy,' he says.

'She' is about female, feline power and, according to Brett, is 'dark and quite sexual and sinister'. For the record, the femme-fatale character in the song is 'a kind of amalgam of women I knew at the time, I suppose. I've always been obsessed with feminine power and, far from seeing women as weak, always viewed them as masterful and dynamic so I tried to give the protagonist in "She" this aura of mutinous, powerful sexuality. There were lots of songs on the first two albums from housewives' perspectives, very much inspired by my mother. Often the characters were trapped and frustrated in those songs, so I consciously decided to invert that, and on *Coming Up* celebrate a different aspect of femininity. I've always loved the sound of the word *she*. It's a sharp and tantalising and charged and sexy word and is almost an onomatopoeia. Although few songwriters will admit it, you can't understate the importance of words as sounds when it comes to writing lyrics. Sometimes we just do things just because it sounds good, and there are occasions when that's okay.'

Brett also suggests that the song 'contains some sort of covert criticism of those who undervalue others just because they have different passions', and, at the risk of sounding like someone who thinks she knows what she's talking about, this is something I had thought all along. What I mean to say is that the song could only be celebratory in nature, since their bawdy and accusatory presence in the song—knowing what we know about Brett's exemplary credentials as an insightful sentient being of the highest order—has to come from a place of empathy and admiration for the female species.

Brett acclaims 'She' as probably his favourite song on *Coming Up*. 'It's dark, uplifting, and menacing, and hasn't dated,' he says. 'I love Richard's descending guitar part and the brutal mid-verse stabs. The rhythm section is stark and nasty, and the strings arrive to prove you wrong just when you think you know what's going to happen next. The lyrics just manage to sit on that sweet spot between oblique and meaningful. It's a place I'm always looking for as a songwriter—somewhere where a narrative is suggested but mystery still exists.' And then he delivers one of his more delightful insights with the suggestion that 'journalists and writers often misunderstand the nature of pop lyrics and want them to speak the same language as prose. Unfortunately, even though they seem to use the same words, they work differently. Journalism is about the text, but music is about the subtext. I often find that I get bored of a song if I know too clearly what it's *about*. Some of my favourite songs I've written have revealed their meanings over decades, and I love that that gives them some sort of life.'

Brett also lets on that he loves the minimalism of the electric guitar sound on the track while admitting that it came about by accident. 'We wrote a demo for the song,' he says, 'and the guitars were hard-panned—which means one guitar was over to the left and one was over to the right—and I remember sitting there one night listening to the demo, and I had a broken stereo so only one of the speakers worked, so I was only listening to one side, and thought, *That sounds brilliant.* These little accidents! We copied that on the actual final recording: we only used the one guitar 'cos it gave the song more space.'

Ed agrees with Brett that 'She' is the best song on *Coming Up* and should have been a single. However, when I tell Neil about

Ed and Brett both loving the song, he suggests that they may like it for different reasons: Brett because it's 'tribal and angular' and Ed because the John Barry string arrangement kicks it up a level and into a cinematic realm. Neil eventually sides with Ed, whilst citing the fact that the band have played it live so much over the years—the song opened the band's live set for much of the *Coming Up* tour and well beyond that—that it's hard to know what he thinks of it as a song or a recording anymore. And, just to clarify things further, Neil is not sure if he can pick out a favourite song on the album, as they've played some songs off it at every gig in the last twenty-five years, so 'they're all part of the furniture'.

Having revealed as much, Neil goes on to hail 'She' as a really great example of Richard's playing style: 'It has its basis in riffs rather than pentatonic noodling, it has intricacies and melodic flair without the bluster that is so hard to avoid for a lead guitarist.' Neil has always regarded Richard as a 'guitarist's guitarist, so talented but without any braggadocio', but Ed's revelation that 'Neil always wants things to be just right, done at his own pace, otherwise he may become distressed or irritated' begs the question: what does that make Neil? To which the answer is surely: the *musicologist's musicologist*.

Neil also maintains that 'She' was yet another song that was just about done before he first rehearsed with the band; he can't remember what he played on it when they first rehearsed it, and he doesn't think he played strings on it until they'd recorded Craig Armstrong's arrangement.

According to Mat Osman, 'She' once featured 'vibes', and I must admit that if I hadn't heard Neil and Richard talking about a Vibraphone earlier in proceedings, I would have had to look the word up as, initially, I thought he was commenting on how cool the song used to be before any of us got to hear it. A cursory glance at the instrument's online profile suggests that I won't be able to fit one into my living room any time soon without injuring one of my children.

Mat also refers to 'She' as a 'clockwork stripper song', and again I am flummoxed for a moment until I remember how the song is performed live: as soon as that first swooping guitar chord kicks in, you can see Brett feeling, *becoming* sexier, veritably slinking across the stage like a cartoon cat with every intention of tempting its predator. It's also live when you see the truth of Buller's suggestion that, rather than being sweeping and luscious, Brett always saw the song as being harder and more mechanical: to wit, when Brett gets wind of that massive drum rhythm intro, he feels a compunction to clap like a sex-crazed metronome.

Richard lets on that 'once the band got hold of the song, it became a stalking, dark piece with tribal drums, all the things we wanted from *Coming Up*. Ed saw a 60s spy thriller potential in it, and it went on a journey during the recording. At one point it was a fairly light but ghostly song, faster than the finished version and featuring vibraphones playing the guitar riff. But we pulled it back into harder, more menacing territory, and once I had found a way to play the descending riff that reflected that menace, it was

115

there. Adding Craig's strings gave it a very Bond-theme feel and worked perfectly. It was a great one to start gigs with, especially with Simon's drum intro loudly and rudely interrupting whatever atmospheric intro music we were using at the time.'

From my standpoint, 'She' strikes me as one of the coolest songs Suede or any other rock band has ever written. I mean, it even seems bored and disinterested in us—which is, surely, the very definition of cool—and aside from the errant misbehaviour it induces in any casual bystander standing in its near vicinity, it also catapults the band themselves into another dimension when performing it. In a live review around the time of release, *Select* magazine appeared to concur with this analysis. 'By the time of "She",' it suggested, 'Brett has once again slammed his mic stand into the stage and is whirling the microphone around his head in an enormous arc that barely misses the heads of Oakes, Osman and Codling in their neo-beatnik costumes of black shirts, black hipsters and black leather jackets.'

I think it's important to point out that 'She' is also a very weird song. Savagely melodramatic in both execution and delivery, it's only after a couple of listens that you realise the chorus is really just a more manically rearranged version of the verse, and then another couple more before you notice you've been singing along to pretty much the same words throughout the entire three and a half minutes of its existence. '*She, walking like a killer / She, another night another pillow,*' sings Brett, completely dispensing with both rhyme and reason for a moment, before the *la-la-las* punctuate proceedings and all hell breaks loose. Continuing apace, Brett mentions some 'nowhere faces' and even some 'nowhere places' until 'No education it's the arse of the nation' suddenly leads us into our female protagonist being bad as well as bored and bony, and you'd be forgiven for thinking—and at the risk of sounding like my mum—She doesn't sound very happy, does she?

Incidentally, about those la-la-las: they're falsetto, of course, deliberately so—think of all those ridiculous doo do-doo do-doo do-do-dos in 'Walk On The Wild Side'—and delivered sarcastically in such a way as to mock the absurdities of the verse/chorus/verse structure in the first place. Naturally, there's nothing absurd about the casually menacing guitar pervading through the song, and 'Nowhere faces / Nowhere places' is Pistols tomfoolery of the highest order.

The oddest couplet on 'She' rhymes 'karma' with 'injecting mar-ij-uana', blurted out in such hilariously contrived fashion that you know there's some serious smirking going on behind the scenes. I have it on good authority that injecting marijuana is not an advisable course of action, even when presented with an absence of all available drugs that would usually do the job. But then again . . . I told you the song was weird.

10

LADIES AND GENTLEMEN, MR GEORGE MICHAEL

"That's a gorgeous coat, said an impossibly good-looking young man standing in a throng of several other impossibly good-looking men who were now crowding around me.

I love the way it hangs on you, he added, and reached over to pick it up off the sofa. He gathered up the garment so that he could see the label.

Oh, Christ, he shouted. *It's River Island!"*

'You can't do a photo session on an E.'

For the seasoned, long-suffering music journalist, there is no less alluring or more uninspiring interview subject than a pop star who only wants to talk about music when tasked with promoting a new record. This is one of the not-so-famous sweeping generalisations that you may have read about in my well-respected book on the subject, *Why Pop Stars Are Less Interesting Than Me And You*, though the British media recognise this suggestion as a self-evident truth in a way that the media in other parts of the world do not.

Naturally, I am not suggesting that the UK is the only country in the world whose media is not controlled by the state, but even in the USA, widely mooted as a hotbed of democracy (mostly by Americans), there is little scope for diversion from the version of the truth promulgated by major record labels and their publicists who are keen to market their product with the least amount of fuss and controversy.

Which brings me to the loveable and eccentric world of George Michael.

I can't pretend that I knew George well, and yet, when I first met him, he said, 'Hello, we have met before—I know you, don't I?' I spent the next couple of hours watching him as if I was an overzealous ex-girlfriend who, not being able to afford a private detective, had now decided to stalk the object of her affections in plain sight. On several further occasions, I noticed that he pretty much said the same thing to everyone he was introduced to. At the time—and I haven't changed my opinion since—I chose to think that this was just his way of being polite, so as to put any new acquaintance at ease. Of course, the cynics amongst you might suggest this was a clever way of enticing people to respond, 'Yes, George, we do know each other, it's so lovely that you remember me, how nice to be reacquainted.' In hindsight, I began to imagine that many of these innocent-enough introductions must have resulted in George being reunited with the vast array of men he had got to know on an intimate basis—but had now forgotten— in some of the more celebrated public spaces around London.

Like a lot of people in the music industry, I was aware that George's interview technique was not your run-of-the-mill Q&A session, and anyone fortunate enough to meet him in the comfort of his north London home was in for a real treat. Of course, you can be assured that any arrangement for an interview with George was no different to any other arrangement for an interview with any other pop star, but the similarities need to be noted nonetheless: the pop star's new album has been looming ever larger on a record company's release schedule for several months and, even though this has only ever manifested itself as a selection of A4 sheets held together by a paper clip, it is now proving to have a tangible significance; at the appropriate juncture, the publicist calls a magazine editor, explaining that George would like to talk about his new record, and a time and place for the interview is agreed upon; subsequently, a copy of the new recordings are dispatched to several hand-picked journalists utilising the most up-to-date means of distribution.

As one of the handpicked journalists, you are more than happy to have been assigned the task of interviewing one of the most enigmatic and intriguing pop stars alive today. Then, when you arrive at George's house—with a list of questions you have been preparing for quite some time—it is perhaps true to say that you have been waiting for an opportunity like this ever since you gate-crashed the profession you'd always dreamed of working in; your father had always criticised your dreams as 'sketchy and without substance', although the connotations of his views only surface on the way to the interview, when you are trying to think about something other than the actual interview itself. As you are waiting for the bus, and then the tube, and finally the hastily arranged taxi that you hail once you realise you are going to be late, you remember the conversation you had when you had dinner with him last week.

'I respect George and the journey he is on,' your father had said, almost as if it was an entirely normal way for a father and daughter to discuss their mutual love for the abstract entity that was George Michael. For a brief, incomprehensible moment, you wonder if your father is about to reveal that he is gay. Then, when he says, 'I even liked the wacky, *laissez-faire*, *sans gravitas* nature of Wham!'s early career—and that includes "Wham Rap" and "Club Tropicana"!' he announces it in such jocular fashion that you know such a revelation is not going to be forthcoming.

'And now, knowing what I know,' he continues, 'and after hearing "Careless Whisper" about a million times, I think he deals with issues of love and regret with a maturity and sensitivity that belies his tender years.'

There's more unexpected discourse, of course—'I think George was so brave to disband Wham! at the height of their fame and success and embark upon a solo career that could have gone horribly wrong like it did for so many before him'—but by this point you have switched off, fast-forwarding to the terrifying reality of the encounter you have ahead of you. Naturally, the terror encompasses the possibility that George won't warm to you and, perhaps, not even regard you as a serious journalist; with the weight of the world on your mind, it's hardly surprising that your father's words could only ever be a mildly amusing distraction, and you just want to get through the encounter with your integrity and some legible notes intact. Then you remember your father saying that he is proud of you and asking whether you could get George to sign something as a memento of the occasion. The thought of asking George to do such a thing makes you cringe.

George's publicist requests that you come to his house in Highgate, and, when you get there, his offer of a drink is accepted so that you don't seem *difficult*. You've barely taken your first sip when he asks if you would like to share a joint. *No*, you say, *that's very kind of you to offer*, but you don't partake of such substances during working hours as it interferes with your capacity to function as a journalist. George immediately rolls the fattest joint you have ever seen. He lights the end and sucks on it like a child who has been waiting several hours for an ice-cream treat.

You are about to ask your first question when the front door opens, and a man—presumably his boyfriend—enters the room and kisses George on the lips. George behaves as you would expect him to behave, hugging his boyfriend efficiently before suggesting that he should go upstairs in order for you and him to have some privacy. The man smiles, kisses George again, and leaves the room.

At the precise moment it seems appropriate to commence the interview, George becomes animated, saying that he is not interested in talking about his new record *or anything remotely connected* to *record company bullshit*; he is only interested in talking about sex and drugs and the reality of his everyday life in north London. Your first thought is . . . *ker-ching*, as you can think of nothing worse than asking George to go through his new record, track by track—presumably like he has done for every other journalist on the current press circuit—so you nod your head in agreement. You are overcome with the feeling that if you had made some kind of objection, George would have carried on as if you weren't even there.

Naturally, you listen open-mouthed as George reveals the extent of the casual sex he has had on Hampstead Heath in the last few weeks—a location you know well and could walk to in a matter of minutes once the interview has come to its natural conclusion. As he recounts the intimate details of the countless frenzied sexual liaisons he has enjoyed with men he has propositioned on the Heath, and in public conveniences—and in public conveniences on the Heath—you wonder how you are meant to respond; whether you should appear nonplussed or unoffended, presuming, that is, that you could even pull off either of these abstract facial expressions.

After an hour, the interview ends, and George shakes your hand before hugging you and kissing you on both cheeks. As you embrace, you feel like you are saying goodbye to a close friend who has just revealed something extremely personal. You suspect you are now exaggerating the significance of your meeting with George and reading far too much into the nuances of his behaviour. As he opens the front door, you hug again, and there is a brief, awkward exchange of words where both of you suggest that you will keep in touch via the official channels, and perhaps even on an unofficial and personal basis thereafter.

* * *

I first met George in 1994, after becoming acquainted with his close friend Brad Branson, an aspiring filmmaker who arrived on the London scene in the early 1990s like a violent, gorgeous gust of wind and an accident waiting to happen. In September that year, Brad had been commissioned to photograph Suede for the cover of *Attitude* magazine—a cover that was part of a press campaign that, since Bernard's abrupt departure several weeks earlier, had now become troublesome beyond belief. I mentioned in an earlier chapter how Brett had refused to let Rankin photograph Suede as a three-piece for the cover of *Select* magazine—since they might thus appear *damaged* somehow—but the *Attitude* article and cover would be a perfect riposte to the doubters, since it would only feature the newly out Suede stick-man Simon Gilbert and the apparently sexually ambivalent/ambiguous Brett Anderson as its cover stars.

Having said that, I didn't attend the session—I must have felt comfortable enough to let Brett and Simon get on with it—but the reports back were so encouraging that Brad was immediately commissioned by Nude Records to take photographs of the whole band—now a four-piece—in the weeks to come. It proved to be the beginning of a beautiful friendship.

The 'official' band photo session occurred during that period in my life when Suede were the kind of press darlings who could commandeer the cover of any UK magazine without bothering to get out of bed—a proposition they liked to confirm whenever the opportunity arose. I had attended so many of their photo sessions in the past that I was now used to the excuses and prevarications associated with their now-famous lateness—I once waited almost an entire day for Brett to arrive for a Nick Knight shoot for *i-D* magazine and was actually astonished when he finally appeared, unflustered and with an apparent lack of concern, just as the clock struck midnight—and when I turned up a couple of hours late for the Nude shoot, I was not surprised to see that the cupboard was bare. I was more than a little shocked, however, when I discovered that the photographer, who had been charged with capturing the essence of my elusive antiheroes on camera, had also failed to materialise.

I am sure you are aware that one of the golden rules of PR is that the photographer and the publicist are expected to arrive on time—you can see why I am not cut out for this PR game—as they are the larks that organised the session in the first place, so this was rather like being late for your own funeral.

Nevertheless, I was intrigued.

I asked one of the stylists if he knew what had happened to the photographer.

'Oh, I don't know,' he said. 'Brad rang about an hour ago and asked if the band were here yet, and when I said *no*, the line went dead.'

A couple of hours later, almost seventy-five percent of the band were already in the process of sneering at the clothes on offer when Brett arrived with a flourish and the kind of runny nose that suggested the flu pandemic in his street had now got out of hand. There was still no sign of the photographer, however, so we started without him.

Some time later—and I don't know how to be exact about these things—I began to get worried that, in the grander scheme of things, my promotional endeavours were as irrelevant as I was, and I could tell the band were getting bored of their make-up ordeal.

I'd also just noticed Mat looking at his watch.

Suddenly, almost as if I had made it happen, the door of the studio burst open, and someone who may or may not have been a photographer stumbled onto the premises. It was Brad. And I couldn't have been more impressed if he'd arrived on a chariot bearing drugs from the Orient.

Which, now I come to think of it, he had.

If I can be honest for a moment—it's the new *me!*—Brad struck me as one of the most handsome guys I had ever seen. Slim but well built, he had dark brown, almost black hair arranged in a frat-boy style that suggested it had taken very little effort to organise but a lifetime to pull off. He appeared to be sweating slightly, although the beads of sweat that I spotted glistening on his impossibly chiselled cheeks and brow were arranged as if he had painted on the artifice just for my benefit.

I am not easily smitten.

And yet I blushed.

No doubt we are all blushing now, but if we can all calm down for a moment, I should tell you that Brad turned out to be as charming as he was handsome. He apologised immediately for being so late before walking over to every member of the band and kissing each one of them on the cheek. I could tell that they were as charmed as I was.

The shoot began to take shape, but there was something of the *anything goes* around proceedings, and I could sense that this was a different kind of photo session. In particular, Brett and Simon seemed to have formed a bond with Brad, and when Brad asked

Brett what it was like to have your photo taken the minute you get out of bed in the morning—and how he managed to get away with looking like a pop star every day of the week—Brett just shrugged and said, 'Well, you can get away with doing a photo session if you've taken a couple of lines, but you can't do one on an E. When you've had an E, you keep looking at yourself in the mirror and laughing, and thinking you look great, and you don't take any notice of the camera. But when you do a line'—he shook his head, and then his shock of hair as if he was a dog emerging from the sea—'well, you know.'

I took this to mean that Brett and Simon had already been talking to Brad about drugs—and, perhaps, that they'd already been taking them together—and all bets were off. A few minutes later, a significant number of lines were somehow arranged on a dressing table in one of the adjoining rooms, and we all started to relax.

Or perhaps to get more uptight.

It's a thin line, even when it isn't.

The session abruptly came to an end, and the band said their goodbyes. As Brad embraced all and sundry—and, after some sweet nothings, Brett and Simon in particular—I could tell that we would all see him again. Then, just as the clothes and make-up, and the people who had brought it all together, slowly disappeared, we found ourselves alone.

'I'm sorry I was late,' said Brad, 'I took some shit and didn't know where I was.'

128

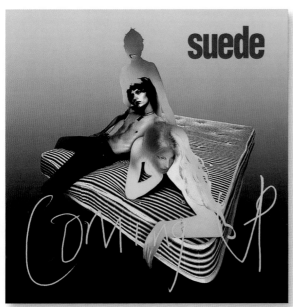

The incredible artwork that art director and graphic designer Peter Saville put together for the *Coming Up* album and all five Top 10 singles that accompanied its release.

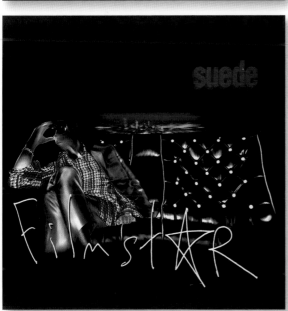

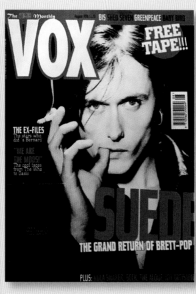

The bill for the 1995 Phoenix festival—the year of the Suede/Dylan headlining mix-up—and some of the front covers that accompanied Suede as they cantered through the drama of the *Coming Up* campaign.

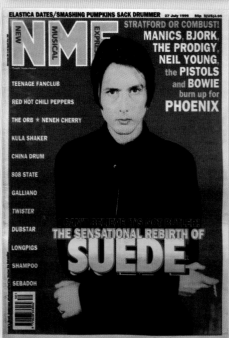

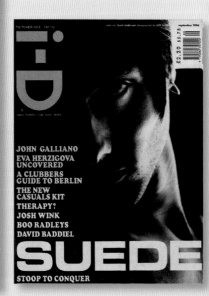

19 October 1996 90p (US)3.95

NEW MUSICAL EXPRESS
N.M.E

DOING THE DUDE:
KULA SHAKER
PJ HARVEY and
OCEAN COLOUR
SCENE LIVE

The beautiful 72 page issue

VIC & BOB:
Laughter! Laughter!
Laughter! Shooting!

GLAMOUR OF THE GODS!
SUEDE
get back in the spotlight

THE BEAUTIFUL SOUTH ★ dEUS ★ REEF ★ CJ BOLLAND ★ BEN LORTON
CHUCK D ★ BABYBIRD ★ AND THE SEARCH FOR THE SPIRIT OF DANCE

VERVE ALBUM REVIEW EMBRACE BENTLEY RHYTHM ACE LIL' KIM

£2.30 NOVEMBER 1997

SELECT

HE'S TAKING YOU 0-VAH

OASIS & RADIOHEAD
LIVE SPECIAL

"I'VE TRIED EVERYTHING"
Suede

THEIR MOST REVEALING INTERVIEW EVER
Brett on Justine, Neil, Bernard,
drugs and his
secret history

FREE CD!
70 MINUTES
OF BRILLIANT
MUSIC

WE REGRET THAT FOR COPYRIGHT REASONS, THIS COMPACT DISC IS NOT AVAILABLE TO READERS OUTSIDE THE UK. SORRY!

Future Shock
THE INSANE WORLD OF TOMORROW

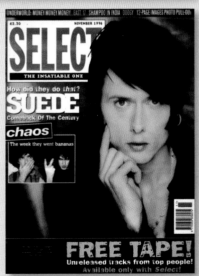

UNDERWORLD: MONEY MONEY MONEY! EAST 17 SHAMPOO IN INDIA DODGY 12-PAGE IMAGES PHOTO PULL-OUT

£2.30 NOVEMBER 1996

SELECT

THE INSATIABLE ONE

How did they do that?
SUEDE
Comeback Of The Century

chaos
The week they went bananas

FREE TAPE!
Unreleased tracks from top people!
Available only with Select!

FREE TATTOOS

Melody
Maker

EVEN BIGGER!
EVEN BETTER!
THE NEW
MAKER
GIG GUIDE

THE MAGNIFICENT V97!
**BLUR, PRODIGY,
KULA SHAKER,
BECK** and more live in
Chelmsford and Leeds

You! Outside! Now!
SUEDE
Brett Anderson gets
Reading to rumble

TRAVIS
HURRICANE #1
SUPERFURRIES
TEENAGE FANCLUB
TANYA DONELLY
KEVIN SPACEY
GRASS-SHOW
DINOSAUR JR
SILVER SUN

5 FREE
TATS!
MANICS!
PRODIGY!
SPICE GIRLS!

I took these shots of Suede in their various guises in Hong Kong on their 1997 *Coming Up* tour. By this point in proceedings, Suede were commandeering such a huge amount of attention over there that you couldn't move for fans sleeping in hotel reception areas, in amongst the mountain of presents they hoped to hand to the band if any of them dared to venture downstairs.

PREVIOUS PAGES A selection of Polaroids that ace lensman Tom Sheehan handed to me whilst photographing the band in the 1990s. Tom actually took the first photograph of Suede that appeared on the cover of *Melody Maker*—under the banner headline 'The best new band in Britain'—in 1992, and I have lost count of the amount of times he has snapped them over the years.

THIS PAGE My *access all areas* pass circa '96, and a live shot of Suede courtesy of Stefano Masselli, taken at Il Palalido, Milan, in November of that year.

I knew exactly what he was talking about—although I pretended I didn't—and listened to his confessions of his heroin abuse as if it was the most normal thing in the world: Brad had been detained earlier that day due to some kind of miscalculation on his part, and that was fine with me.

I think I may have convinced Brad that I didn't really care what drugs he took, and we began to discuss the possibility of him shooting Suede for their next album campaign. As we spoke, I noticed that he didn't seem remotely interested in the photographic paraphernalia associated with the session we had recently abandoned, all of which was now congregated on a bench in the middle of the room. I could only presume that one of his 'people' would be picking everything up, after we had finished off the last remnants of the cocaine left over from the affairs of the day.

Naturally, Brad didn't have any 'people', and, midway through the conversation, he walked over to the bench in the middle of the room, rescuing his tatty-looking camera and slinging it over his shoulder, the clumsiness of this action making us both laugh. Hurriedly, we exchanged phone numbers so that we could meet up to discuss how we could work together again, although as the Nude session turned out to be something of a disaster, this prospect turned out to be a pipe dream: my instincts had been correct, and Brad had indeed become good friends with at least fifty percent of the band by the time I met him. In retrospect, I have no idea how Brad managed to point his camera anywhere near the band in those few hours, and my initial suspicions were confirmed when I received only one black-and-white shot of the band—put together as a composite of individual shots—several weeks after I had expected to see a much larger selection of colour photographs. No doubt, Brad had made yet another miscalculation about the need to provide any pictures at all, but I forgave him, nonetheless.

A week after the Nude session, Brad turned up at my office, presumably as a consequence of him not being able to get hold of me on a phone that I kept in a sock drawer in my office. He looked as gorgeous as ever, and we decided to meet at Soho House the next day.

At Soho House, Brad and I got horrendously drunk and told each other the story of our lives. Mine was uneventful enough, but it turned out that Brad had been brought up in Los Angeles by the notoriously reclusive Hollywood movie diva Gloria Swanson. When pressed on the subject of his upbringing, however, Brad would casually refer to the experience as if it was no more or less unusual than being raised by wolves in the Alaskan wilderness. I hung onto his every word as if he was from a time and place that I could only ever dream of inhabiting.

Brad told me that, as a child, he had become obsessed with Hollywood films and musicals of the 1930s and 1940s. Then, at the age of seventeen, through some kind of serendipity, and whilst still living in LA, he had somehow arranged a 'chance' meeting with Swanson that resulted in him being offered a part-time job as her personal assistant. He never fully explained the depth of the relationship they shared, but he did say that he loved listening to the countless stories she told about her insane life in Hollywood. I could tell he was a true child of *Hollywood's Golden Age*.

Or, at least, that he wanted to be.

I was so moved by Brad's pronouncements that I immediately invited him back to the Highgate apartment I shared with Sophie, my Second Proper Girlfriend. No doubt I wanted her to meet him, and for both of us to hear more about his life in Los Angeles, although I must admit, that I also wanted him to come back so that he could see me dressed as my favourite character from *The Stepford Wives* movie—a close run thing between two of the wives played by Nanette Newman and Katherine Ross—and so that I could utter the phrase so beloved of Ms Swanson: 'Mr DeMille, I'm ready for my close-up.' Or perhaps more appropriately, 'I'll just die if I don't get this recipe,' more commonly associated with Ms Newman. My SPG was now used to the countless idiosyncrasies associated with the process of going out with the likes of me, and, on this occasion, she might even be relieved that the dress she had bought for me had now proven to be a useful addition to my wardrobe.

Brad's other obsession—apart from me, and some bit-part player called Gloria Swanson—was the English occultist, magician, poet, painter, and sorcerer Aleister Crowley. Brad clearly knew far too much about 'the wickedest man alive'—as he was hailed during his lifetime—for me to ever feel comfortable talking about him, and I could tell that Brad sensed my unease. Or perhaps I had indicated my lack of interest somehow. Either way, Brad took every single opportunity to let me know that he thought Crowley was the most maligned man in recent history, and that he felt compelled to right this wrong.

From this point onwards, Brad introduced me and my Second Proper Girlfriend to a world as equidistant from reality as my own experience of that overrated state of being, and yet his world seemed far more glamorous and interesting than anything I had seen during my travels around the music business. He seemed to be intimately associated with everyone working in the fashion scene in London, and we began to attend fashion shows together, meeting and greeting the kind of fabulous people I had no inclination to pursue intimate friendships with. If it's true to say I was intimidated by the casual beauty of my newfound acquaintances then I should also stress they were similarly intimidated by mine—ha!—although, you should know that this was only ever manifested as some kind of idle curiosity on their part. By which I mean to say that most people Brad introduced me to couldn't work out why he was hanging out with the likes of a girl like me, before agreeing to the possibility that I was Brad's new squeeze and someone who just looked like a girl.

Brad was profoundly homosexual to such a degree that he believed everyone in the world to be homosexual—or at least if not homosexual then at least as homosexual as he was. Which was pretty homosexual, when I come to think of it. Indeed, Brad's approach to homosexuality reminds me of an episode of my favourite US sitcom, *Frasier*. The episode, entitled 'The

Doctor Is Out', starts off with Frasier being introduced to Roz's new boyfriend, Barry (played by David Murray), a young and handsome-enough gym junkie whom Frasier is convinced is gay after he refers to his own body as 'a church', Roz already having mentioned that he has edited her closet and thrown out her most embarrassing item—culottes. In the next scene, Frasier follows Roz's boyfriend into a gay bar called Bad Billy's, where he is recognised as a local personality with the result that he is outed live on his next afternoon radio slot on KACL, the Seattle-based station that provides the bedrock to most of the activities surrounding the show's main characters. Later that same day, he bumps into a flamboyant opera director called Alistair Burke (played by Patrick Stewart) who is now romantically interested in Frasier due to our intrepid hero's apparent change of sexual orientation. Frasier—at his most pompous and elitist—becomes over-enamoured with the possibility of becoming one half of a power couple (with Stewart) and the pair embark upon an ill-advised companionship of sorts. As the relationship develops, Frasier invites Stewart to his Eliot Bay Towers apartment to meet his family, where hilarity ensues: Frasier's father, Martin, is perplexed when Stewart arrives at the apartment, as indeed are Frasier's brother Niles and Daphne, who is introduced to Stewart as Niles's expectant wife. It is now Stewart's turn to be perplexed, and when he takes a call from his close friend Placido Domingo, suggesting that he and Frasier have been invited to Madrid, Frasier, for our benefit more than anyone else's, says, 'He's taking me to Madrid!'

'You just met him last week. What's going on? He kissed you,' says Martin.

'He is a man of the theatre, he kisses everyone,' says Frasier. 'Anyway, it is not as if he is the first gay friend I have ever had.'

'He is the first friend you've had who thinks you're gay too,' suggests Niles.

'He does not think I am gay,' replies Frasier.

To which Niles retorts, 'He thinks I'm gay, and I'm standing next to my pregnant wife.'

Which is exactly what Niles would have said about Brad if he'd met him under similar circumstances.

My Second Proper Girlfriend was convinced that Brad was in love with me, but I was more convinced that we simply shared a love of music and cocaine. During one late-night drink-and-drugs session at our Highgate apartment, after my SPG had given up the ghost and retired to bed, Brad cornered me—if I remember rightly, we were pressed up against the drapes masquerading as curtains that had been pulled shut to prevent the unwelcome presence of the rising sun—grasped me round the waist, and thrust his lips towards me in an attempt at an embrace. I felt his unfeasibly rough, early morning stubble— is this the true meaning of a five o'clock shadow?—rubbing against my smooth, cherubic cheeks and recoiled more than was appropriate or even necessary.

'Sorry Brad,' I said, 'I am not into guys.'

'Of course you are,' he laughed. 'You must be. Everyone is. And look at the way you look and dress. Why would you fancy girls?'

'I don't know,' I said, wondering why any girl should fancy any other girl, and whether I should tell him a long story. He knew my long story anyway, so there didn't seem any point in telling it all over again. Particularly as I could hear my SPG raising her eyebrows in the room down the corridor.

The long night became ever more morning whilst seamlessly morphing into something you could only acknowledge as existence at its basest level. This was a time in the day when rash thoughts and even rasher decisions are made to call people who might still be awake and able to deliver the means for keeping people awake for even longer. Eventually, Brad and I collapsed on the sofa together and waited for sleep to come.

Not long after our brief flirtation, and in the midst of a frantic and wonderful friendship, Brad invited me to accompany him to a Vivienne Westwood fashion show. The event took place on a Sunday afternoon in central London in a fancy restaurant now set to host an even more ludicrous collection of individuals than usual. You can guess that if the restaurant had been asked to cater for the event—there weren't any canapes, just champagne and cocktails—our reluctant diners would have picked at their food with that sense of privilege that makes chefs and restaurant owners question why they have chosen a profession that divides and conquers with such carefree abandon.

When Brad and I arrived, I was particularly struck by the fact that everyone in the entire room appeared not to have slept for several days. The show itself seemed of little note, except that I immediately fell in love with an unusual swimsuit I could see being modelled by one of the women on the catwalk. It appeared to be made out of wool—or, at the very least, elaborately crocheted in a fashion that I had never seen before on a swimsuit. Or on any other item of clothing, for that matter.

I asked Brad if he knew how I could buy such an item, and he went off to talk to a member of the Westwood entourage who might be able to help. After a few minutes he returned with an extremely thin, well-manicured young man who looked me up and down in a way that I had never been looked up and down before.

Eventually, the well-manicured young man said, 'You were the one who wanted to know about the bikini, yes?'

I nodded in agreement.

'That's not even a real item of clothing,' he continued. 'We only produced it for the show so we could demonstrate how something as simple as a swimsuit can be as beautiful and desirable as a piece of clothing as a skirt or a dress. Did you really think we were going to make it commercially available?' He made this last comment as if it was the most obvious statement in the world and he had never met anyone as stupid and misguided as me.

'It's completely impractical,' he added. 'It's made of wool, for fuck's sake! It would be useless if you wore it to swim in the sea, or in a swimming pool.' He began to laugh, and I wished there was a way I could leave without anyone noticing. *I just died*, I might have said, if I was a card-carrying member of the fashion world.

The young man went off to deal with more pressing matters and Brad, noticing my discomfort, asked if I wanted to leave.

'No, I'm fine,' I said. 'I only asked about the swimsuit because I thought my girlfriend would look great in it, and I wanted her to feel special and that she owned a piece of clothing that wasn't available and on sale anywhere. I didn't expect to be humiliated.'

Brad assured me that the 'notorious bitch' who'd been kind enough to talk to me had a habit of putting people in their place. This seemed likely enough, and by the time we both sat down to watch another group of casually gorgeous boys and girls sashaying down the catwalk—unashamedly advertising a further selection of impractical outfits never to be on sale to the general public—I began to feel less like someone who didn't deserve to be part of such a self-evidently exalted fashion elite.

The catwalk routine ended, and I found myself sitting on a sofa amongst a group of models-slash-designers who had inadvertently ended up sitting with the likes of me. After several minutes where no one appeared to speak—or, if they did, it was in a hushed whisper and in a secret language I would never be privy to—I finally felt comfortable enough to remove the long, fake-fur-collared, dark brown suede coat I had persuaded myself to wear for the occasion. I placed the coat on the sofa beside me and announced that I was going to the bathroom.

'That's a gorgeous coat,' said an impossibly good-looking young man standing in a throng of several other impossibly good-looking men who were now crowding around me.

'I love the way it hangs on you,' he added, and reached over to pick it up off the sofa. He gathered up the garment so that he could see the label.

'Oh, Christ,' he shouted. 'It's River Island!'

As he said this, I noticed a look of horror on his face, as if he had just picked up and smelt something unidentifiably awful off the carpet. I began my journey to the bathroom, aware that this latest faux pas would sit inside the portfolio of shame now being collated as evidence that I should be excluded from all forthcoming Vivienne Westwood shows still yet to be scheduled.

Some moments later, after I had successfully ventured back from the bathroom, the small group of models-slash-designers with whom I had been sitting seemed much less gorgeous than when I had left them. I suggested to Brad that we should make our excuses and leave. Five minutes later, we were sitting in a pub around the corner, discussing the merits of hanging out with the kind of people you wouldn't normally consider hanging out with. At this point, I almost loved him.

Brad and I left the pub at a horrendously late hour on Monday morning. In the cab, in a rare moment of weakness, on the way to a house that neither of us lived in—nor knew anyone that did—Brad admitted that he only tolerated the fashion scene as a means of entry into a world where he could photograph people who belonged in the kinds of magazines that would confirm his status as the kind of photographer who had a future in Britain. I felt there was an unspoken agreement that Brad's endeavours were

138

borne out of the necessity to finance his chosen lifestyle—or the lifestyle that had been chosen for him—and the heroin habit that had pursued him across the pond.

Funnily enough, I lost my appetite for fashion people after the Westwood show and, whenever Brad mentioned one was around the corner, I feigned illness or a clash of schedules. After a while, he stopped asking. However, when Brad proposed that my Second Proper Girlfriend and I should meet his good friend George, I found myself agreeing with his outrageous suggestion.

I heard from several people who should have known better that the Brad and George 'good friends' tag was something of a misnomer: Brad and George had had a fling at some point, and George still harboured romantic feelings towards Brad. Unfortunately, for reasons that never became apparent, the sentiments were not reciprocated. Brad loved George to bits, but he wasn't interested in pursuing any further intimacy, or a romantic relationship of any kind. Subsequently, I would learn that George's song 'Cowboys And Angels', released as long ago as 1991, concerned a love triangle with Kathy Jeung (who was in love with George) and Brad (who wasn't), and was ultimately his way of coping with his unrequited love for Brad.

Some weeks after the Westwood show, Brad invited my SPG and me to accompany him to the Albert Hall to see Elton John, a performance that would include George appearing on stage with Elton to perform a couple of numbers towards the end of the show. All three of us agreed that we could think of nothing better to do on a school night.* We arranged to meet at a pub as close to the Albert Hall as possible, and one with the least probability of bumping into anyone associated with the music business or the drab nature of our miserable existence.

When we arrived at the pub, I could tell Brad had already been partying, but as my SPG and I were in a similar state of confusion, it seemed churlish to mention anything. We drank and smoked as if in a war zone with no chance of supplies being replenished by the authorities, and before long we had left the pub and were comfortably situated in what I suspected to be the most expensive and exclusive box in the Albert Hall. Naturally, no doubt due to the state I was in—*Illinois!* I hear you cry—I felt no sense of shame or privilege, and, after a brief respite to exchange pleasantries with the other characters unfortunate enough to be in the same box as

---

* Many years later, after the birth of my children, I would come to use this term to explain why I couldn't stay out until 5am. In those days, however, we were still young enough to call our so-called work, *school*. Of course, it was much more fun than school, but some things never change: when I regularly used to turn up several hours—or sometimes several days—late for work, my business partner, John, regularly used to ask, 'Why are you so late?'

To which I would reply, 'It was the Australian General Election last night. Doh!'

And then again: 'It's nearly 2pm, what's the excuse this time?'

'Peru versus Chile. Don't you know anything!' (I found that Denmark versus Norway worked just as well.)

And finally—except it never was finally: 'Where were you yesterday?'

'Jesus. It was Greek Easter Sunday. Don't you know what that means?'

It is perhaps for this reason alone, that I always saw John as my boss, although you can see what a pleasant experience it was to work in the same office as me in those days.

us, we decided it was as good a time as any to start chopping out lines on the edge of the balcony.

The show was engaging enough, but it couldn't have been the best show I had seen that month, as I was now in the habit of seeing about a hundred not-yet-famous-but-brilliant bands every day of the week. I remember the Albert Hall crowd lapping everything up, in the way that all crowds that have paid over the odds and organised babysitters and gentle hangovers for the school run will always lap everything up.

After a suitable period of reflection—and despite the fact that the effects of Brad's over-intuitive coke were now making me lose the power of reason—I became dimly aware that Elton was finishing one of his more flamboyant songs with a flourish.

Something was about to happen.

The room fell silent.

I heard Elton uttering several sentiments that could only have been momentous and moving—although it could just as easily be someone else speaking loudly in the same building, possibly on a raised platform or stage of some kind—and so I decided to pay attention.

'This song has a very special meaning for me,' proclaimed Elton, with a sincerity that I could never hope to imitate. 'It's called "Don't Let The Sun Go Down On Me".'

There was a palpable change in the atmosphere in the room, and I heard the woman behind me gasp at the importance of the occasion.

'Ladies and Gentlemen, Mr George Michael,' said Elton.

At the exact juncture that our Most Famously Flamboyant And Bespectacled National Treasure uttered these immortal words—a phrase of such gravity that I could barely assimilate its implications—George made his entrance onto the stage. He looked magnificent, like some kind of award-winning horse one could only admire from a distance. And, since you ask, it wasn't just his beautifully manicured, coiffured hair that made me think so.

On stage, Elton and George acknowledged one another as only the truly famous can, before Elton began to play his piano, the intro to the song gently reminding us we were now in the presence of the genius that had created so many special moments in our childhoods.

I'd like to be able to tell you that my unique sensitivity to the poignancy of the occasion was a contributory factor in my decision to pull a bottle of champagne out of my handbag and immediately pop it open, but, alas, no: the bottle was perhaps not from a vintage that likes to behave itself anyway, and, with spectacular abandon, immediately shot its cork over the edge of the balcony and down to the depths of the elaborate proceedings unfolding below. From our vantage point, I could see that the cork had a life of its own and was now flinging itself with the kind of speed and trajectory one usually associates with objects of a more substantial nature.

With perfect asymmetry, I watched the cork land on the keys

of Elton's piano. Then, almost as if aware of the damage it was now causing, the offending appendage hurled itself sideways, before finally spiralling down to the depths of the floor beneath Elton's shoes. I noticed that each shoe was platformed.

To his credit, Elton, who was presumably used to such inveterate, ill-advised behaviour, merely glanced up at our box, noting the presence of Brad and perhaps even the distressed version of the young woman standing next to him, clutching a bottle of champagne. Aside from this gently administered glance and perhaps a tiny sigh that could only have been recognised by a seasoned observer such as myself, Elton showed very little emotion, other than one you would expect to be associated with a special song sung with a special person to a special bunch of people.

After the concert ended, our exemplary behaviour must have counted for something, as we were immediately invited to have dinner with George and his entourage. Naturally, the successful intake of food had not been shortlisted as one of my long-term goals, but then again, neither was sitting around a table in a brightly lit restaurant. Indeed, the prospect filled me with dread.

By this point, Brad and I were indefensibly drunk and coke-addled beyond the usual bounds of acceptance, but as soon as I nodded my head in agreement, I found myself exiting the Albert Hall, accompanied by several accomplices who bore striking resemblances to Brad, my SPG, and a considerable number of bright sparks I hoped I wouldn't bump into again. After a muddled conversation with someone who may or may not have been George's manager, or his bodyguard—aren't they always the same person?—we all ended up at a restaurant where George was said to be holding court. At such a late hour, it seemed unnaturally crowded, but this was the least surmountable of my problems after I noticed the narrow, steep set of stairs I was now expected to descend in heels that would have unsteadied a supermodel. Naturally, I survived the ordeal—I have the kind of pins a supermodel would die for—to such an extent that I still speak of potential catastrophes like this to this day.

When my SPG and I were successfully underground, Brad beckoned both of us over to a table and introduced us to George.

Right on cue, George said, 'We have met before, haven't we?'

As a matter of fact, I thought, *we have*. And, for the first time in our recently unrequited acquaintance, *you are right*.

And then he said, 'Which one is Sophie?'

Plus ça change, plus c'est la même chose, I thought. In actual fucking French.

Later that night—although I don't see how it could have got any later—my SPG and I ended up sitting next to George, and we got on famously. Of course, he was getting on more famously than we were, but I fail to see why this should change the way I should view our relationship. The following week, Brad and I ended up at another restaurant with George, and it was the first time that George didn't suggest that we knew each other, or that we had met before. I was almost traumatised: was this because he knew we *had* met before, and he knew who I was? Indeed, had

I now spent enough time in his field of vision that he no longer felt the need to pretend we were new acquaintances? Or had he come to the conclusion that, since we had never slept together on Hampstead Heath—does anyone actually sleep there after they have slept together?—there was little point in entertaining the possibility that we were likely to.

For the next few months, Brad remained oblivious to the lack of sexual frisson that George and I had now begun to enjoy as a very real thing. Naturally, Brad and I carried on regardless, and since Brad was now living in Soho—where else?—we spent several more nights out together at Soho House. One evening, after I mentioned that my best friend, Rupert, owned a garage specialising in Citroen DSs, Brad became adamant that he wanted to get his hands on one. I arranged for Brad to meet Rupert at Soho House the following evening, but when we arrived Brad was already there, sitting with George at a table. We were all briefly introduced, before George disappeared to pursue more interesting adventures.

As soon as George had left, Brad made one of his many visits to the bathroom.

My friend, Rupert, said, 'What does that lovely guy, George, do for a living?'

Brad ended up buying a DS after asking George to provide the £15,000 he needed to buy it. The car turned out to be the most impractical vehicle you could own in London whilst simultaneously having an impressively expensive heroin habit and no tangible means of earning enough money to finance a regular parking facility. One night, not long after he had taken possession of the DS, Brad got drunk and distracted enough to abandon his car on a double yellow line. The next day, and for several days after this, I kept asking him if he knew when he had last seen his car, but he was convinced that he had never owned it in the first place. I knew that the car must have been towed to a car pound within the first few hours of being abandoned, but when I eventually managed to get Brad to admit that he actually did own a car—but had forgotten where he had left it—he couldn't get his head round the fact that the longer the car stayed in the pound, the more he would have to pay to get it back. After several conversations, during which Brad held his head in his hands whilst simultaneously bending the same head down to snort the lines of coke he had placed in front of him, I persuaded him that I should call my friend to see if he could rescue the car. Several days later, after several thousand pounds had been handed over at the pound, Brad got his car back.

And so it went on. Brad and I remained an unlikely couple and yet not a couple at all, both grateful for our confused and confusing friendship. I am sure that we were both aware that our relationship was doomed to failure, and before long we would have to pursue different paths. Naturally, almost imperceptibly, over the next few months we began to drift apart—just as Brad and George seemed to be doing. One day, when Brad told me that he needed to go back to LA to finish writing his Aleister Crowley script—and perhaps find someone brave and famous enough to direct it—I knew we would never see each other again. We were standing in the kitchen of my Highgate apartment, and I can honestly say it was the only time we spent together when neither of us was high. No doubt we were waiting for someone or something to arrive, but we both cried nonetheless. Or at least I did.

A few days later, Brad left for LA, and we never spoke again. In 2010, when he came back to London to photograph George, he never got in touch. And even though a part of me wanted George and Brad to become even greater friends and find some deeper kind of love, another part of me wonders whether, when Brad arrived back in the UK and met George for dinner, George celebrated the reunion by announcing, 'Hello, I know you, don't I? We have met before.'

* * *

Brad died of cancer on December 13, 2012. He was forty-nine years old.

SIDE B ...

11

SEX AND GLUE

"There are more drug references on 'Beautiful Ones' than on any other Suede song I can think of ..."

'*That is definitely not a single.*'

Side B of *Coming Up* kicks off with 'Beautiful Ones', a song populated with a procession of freaks 'based on friends', says Brett, although he also admits his fascination with 'beautiful losers' is probably down to a misguided sense of romance. 'In a song, you can actually take a bad situation and turn it into something good. It's quite a karmic process. You can take all the shit in the world and stick it through this filter, stick it into the blender, and with the right ingredients you get something great.'

'It's odd how when songs become really popular you feel, as a writer, less ownership of them,' Brett tells me. '"Beautiful Ones" was one of those that over the years has just taken on a life of its own. It's like a really successful kid who grows up and becomes some sort of high-flyer: you never need to worry about them and so your attention as a parent becomes focussed on the more damaged members of your brood.'

The original title for 'Beautiful Ones' was 'Dead Leg', after Mat Osman dropped Richard Oakes at his flat with the jokey threat, 'If you don't write us a Top 10 single, I'm going to give you a dead leg!' Richard had several other working titles like 'Wedgie' and 'Chinese Burn' based on childhood tortures, but, sometime later, he turned up at Brett's flat and handed a cassette over. 'I gave him a cup of tea whilst me and Alan were partying,' said Brett. 'I was swaying but I thought it was a really good riff and all I had to do was pin a melody to it.'

When he'd stopped swaying, Brett tore a few pages out of his notebook and started singing. 'It was a funny afternoon,' he recalls, 'and there was a bit of insanity coming through as I was in a sweatbox of a studio with no air conditioning.' That studio was the tiny room that he and Richard had started writing in. 'When you build a studio,' Brett adds, 'you build a room within a room, so that little box room in Chesterton Road was six inches smaller than the room and contained me, Richard, and Alan and a couple of other people.' It wasn't long before 'Dead Leg' became 'Beautiful Scum', a song 'about my marginal life and the insane world we live in on the edges of society and the people we know and the beautiful underbelly of London'.

The song itself, adds Richard, 'is a weird little light piece that I wrote one evening after a rehearsal.' He confirms that Mat did indeed give him an ultimatum that mentioned 'dead legs' if he didn't write a hit, but once he'd written and demoed the song, he'd turned up at Chesterton Road in the midst of a party that suggested Brett and Alan had been up for several days.

'I had my friend Peter Field staying with me,' says Richard, 'so we both went over to Brett's. It's amazing that Alan has video of that afternoon'—footage of the occasion surfaced in Mike Christie's superb documentary *The Insatiable Ones*—'when the four of us were crammed into Brett's studio, sweating and playing the song over and over again so Brett could refine his ideas. God knows what Peter made of it, but I'm glad he was there to witness the birth of the song, and also what working life was like for me in 1995!'

Richard confesses to the demo having 'nothing in common with the other hard-hitting songs we'd been writing, but Brett instinctively saw pop potential in it and wrote a very infectious melody over the top and little snippets of phrases and imagery—painting with words, almost. He didn't like my original chorus for it, so he originally had a middle eight and ended on the chorus, but Ed thought the verse melody was the real gold in the song and wanted to end with the verse but with *la-las* over the top, which worked amazingly well. And Neil chiming in with the occasional harmony over certain words and phrases also gave the song a unique edge. It took forever to get the guitar intro to sound good, but it's always like that with busy parts. Again, the rhythm track is fairly different for a Suede song, and when we play it live it's much more driving and aggressive. I can't really remember what I was aiming at when I came up with the original music, but it evolved into one of our most powerful and best-known songs. I guess the planets aligned.'

'Like many of the songs on *Coming Up*,' says Neil, 'the hooky backing vocals provide a poppy scope to it all. That *la-la-la* coda is a standout crossover moment. Lyrically, like "Trash", the song is a call to arms, an outsider anthem, Suede's equivalent of Johnny Strabler's *Whaddya got?*'

Brett suggests that 'Beautiful Ones' is 'like most good pop songs as it features lyrics that don't have a great deal of depth—the strength of the song is all about the melody and the guitar hook. Again, I'm using words as sounds, but I think this particular technique is interesting. It's much more of a sort of stream-of-consciousness approach rather than a narrative approach. I'm just throwing words and phrases around. Hopefully though they paint a kind of impressionistic sketch of the unhinged life Alan and I used to lead in the mid-90s. It's supposed to be a kind of scruffy portrait of the cavalcade of weirdos that used to stumble up and down our stairs at the time, but the intention is to give them a kind of dignity despite everything. It was designed as a kind of defiant celebration of otherness, and originally the song was actually called "Beautiful Scum", before my business brain kicked in and I saw the potential for something that connected to a wider public.'

As recently as 2021, Brett was telling the *Insatiable Ones* fanzine that 'you can talk about inspiration points but pinning a concrete *meaning* to a song is just so reductive, so I'd rather not bother'. That 'words as sounds' idea rings ever louder as Brett—during the course of the same interview—suggested that sometimes he doesn't even know what the songs are about. 'I quite like that,' he maintained, 'how the meaning reveals itself sometimes over the years. Some songs obviously have concrete meanings for the writer, but some will just be impressionistic. I often throw phrases and words around to create a sense of atmosphere and make no apologies for that. It's like painting with different colours; you're learning to create a response in the listener by evoking feelings which aren't always married to meaning. The writer has to let go of the song at some point and give it to the listener who breathes new life into it with their own subjective interpretation and at that

152

point the artist relinquishes their own personal dominion.'

In an interview with *Vox* magazine in 1996, Brett confessed that when he first wrote 'Beautiful Ones', 'I didn't quite know what it was and was quite shocked, because it doesn't fit into how I'd been writing before.' In the same interview, he elaborated further on his songwriting process: 'I take bits of everyday life and try and make them into something good. It's quite a karmic process. One of the great things revealed about writing is being able to take something that's considered to be a bad experience and turning it into something that's good—a pop song—which all my favourite bands like Pet Shop Boys and Bowie have also done to some extent. I don't think I've glamorised it. I just try to go beyond being so negative.'

'Beautiful Ones' is much more verse-based—famously, inevitably, producer Ed Buller implicitly understood this to such an extent during the recording process that he never really saw it as a contender for single release—than your traditional Suede fare.* In more convivial times, Brett has admitted to 'a Suede vocabulary. I do use a lot of the same words. I'd like to have a patent on them so if anyone else uses a word or phrase, it sounds like they're ripping off a Suede word.' Appropriately enough, the phrase that kickstarts shenanigans—'*High on diesel and gasoline*'—is not really

---

* Come to think of it, a traditional Suede Fayre is something I would happily pay to attend—admittedly, there'd be more Bernard Butler lookalikes than was either appropriate or necessary, but there'd be Morris dancing to early Suede B-sides and absolutely no food whatsoever.

supposed to be about drugs at all, but is instead 'a metaphor for city madness, the pollution in cities is turning everyone into a loony by way of involuntary insanity'. When people first heard the song, Brett was quick to point out that you'd have to be pretty stupid to sniff petrol. As stupid, presumably, as you'd have to be to inject marijuana.

'"Beautiful Ones" had something about it, especially that guitar intro,' says Saul Galpern. As it turns out, *that* guitar intro, according to Ed Buller, was one of the hardest things to get right. 'There was a melody in there but also a low note, and it's a bit too busy,' he says, 'so as soon as you added distortion, it turned into a mess.' In the end, there's something of a country riff about it, but, as Saul points out, even though 'the verses were strong, it didn't really take off until they got in to record it and brought the chorus out and the hooky *la-la-las* at the end which were missing from the original demo. Those *la-la-las* were the cherry on top, and Ed didn't rate it until then—but all credit to him for pushing Brett all the way.'

Concurrently, Ed is canny enough to let me know that his original opinion that 'Beautiful Ones' had little prospect of ever being a single may have emerged due to him being very generous with his 'absurd statements.' Whatever the truth of the matter, his initial pronouncements on the subject became something of an albatross around his neck (if there's a mixed metaphor in there, it's all my own doing), as the subsequent success of the song as a single, coupled with the love it continues to engender amongst the extended Suede family—by which I mean to say, everyone in the world who loves Suede as much as I do—surely contrasts with the received view on the subject by the UK government at the time.

Further to his defence, Ed maintains that there were so many songs competing for attention around the time of recording—specifically 'Money' and 'Young Men'—that he didn't know where to turn. 'The verse was hooky but the chorus just didn't work,' he says now. 'And to be honest, by the time we were listening to songs as potential singles, we were in a Hollywood studio frame of mind, and I didn't want the band to be a cliché.'

Richard Oakes now suggests that Ed actually *did* see it as a single—he just wanted it a bit faster. 'When we refused,' he says, 'he got frustrated. Hence that bit of video.' Here, Richard is referring to footage of Ed and the band arguing about the song. 'Arguments like that happened on a daily basis,' says Richard.

Neil often finds himself positioned midway between several contrasting views on Suede songs, and 'Beautiful Ones' is no exception. 'Ed only came to think of it as a single when we added the *la-la-la* coda,' he says, 'and to be fair to him, that's the moment at every gig when the crowd is at its wildest.' There's not a lot of keyboards on 'Beautiful Ones' beyond some synth in the intro and a Mellotron in the chorus, he notes, 'but from the first time I put the demo in my cassette player in my tiny kitchen in Crouch End, I thought there was something special about it. Most of my memories of recording the song revolve around getting the intro/verse guitar riff to sound right and getting the skippy drums to groove. The drumbeat and the accompanying conga rhythm is pretty un-Suede-like, and Simon plays a different beat when we play the song live.'

Lyrically, 'Beautiful Ones' conjures up several more apposite reflections on matters unusual. '*Shaking their bits to the hits*' somehow correlates to Brett's assertion that 'music is a soundtrack to the city where you have Radio 1 and Capital Radio blaring out from building sites'; '*drag acts, drug acts, suicides*' is a phrase half-inched from 'Going Blond', an early Suede tune that never saw the light of day, from when Elastica lead singer and Suede co-founding member Justine Frischmann was still a going concern. You should know that this mutual exchange of ideas, and the original lyric—'*See that druggy act, AC/DC drag act / On the wires in the sky tonight*'—actually surfaced on 'See That Animal', the B-side to Elastica's 'Connection', released in October 1994.

The avalanche of words continues apace with '*In your dad's suits you hide*', which Brett explains away by suggesting, 'We all grew up with hand me down gear and jumble stuff and wore your dad's suit to the local disco'; and more familiar jocularity such as '*Psycho for sex and glue*'. The latter may be 'cheap ways of getting out of it', but the kiss-off that follows—'*Lost it to Bostik, yeah*'—is just about my favourite line on the whole record.

There are more drug references on 'Beautiful Ones' than on any other Suede song I can think of, and, when pressed on the matter, Brett says he spends 'a lot of time writing after I've been on a binge and I'm feeling quite down the next day.' We know the song emanated from the depths of one of these binges, but it's good to know that Brett leaves his 'Dictaphone by the side of the bed, because I often write some of my best stuff when I'm waking up, so you let half a dream into the song, let your subconscious take over. And my brain would probably take over. And my brain would probably be very different if I hadn't taken a lot of drugs over the years. I'd probably be a lot more boring.'

Just so we can put a lid on our enquiries, Brett suggests that 'a lot of the scattered imagery in, for instance, "Killing Of A Flashboy", or the stream of consciousness in "Beautiful Ones"—a string of words that don't have any coherent meaning, that don't belong in any neat little story, that starts with an introduction and ends in a punchline—come from this fidgety, uneasy feeling that drugs create.' And so, if you can say one thing about 'Beautiful Ones', it's that it never gives up. Naturally, the song's celebratory 'shaved heads' and 'rave heads' immediately spring to mind, before we get what we came for: our beautiful ones. Herein, the Greatest Chorus Of All Time—musically, just a continuation of the verse—laughs in the face of those *you're not a single* accusations, before morphing into a better-late-than-never, musical interface, featuring several delicious *Young Americans*-era Bowie inflexions.

The song reaches a natural climax with a fanfare of *la-la-las* worthy of the run-out grooves of Elton John's 'Crocodile Rock'—or perhaps even Iggy Pop's 'The Passenger'—Buller cleverly choosing to evaporate these allusions to pop grandiloquence into the distance.

Hey, it was too good to end anyway.

12

VIOLENCE

"On 'She', Brett managed to smuggle *No stimulation in this privatisation* past the Syntax Police—of which I am an honorary member—without eliciting further comment, but 'Starcrazy' is a step into the unknown..."

'We send him out to entertain the female fans, bike him over to Smash Hits, work him viciously. He may be very fresh and appealing now but in five years he's going to look decrepit and the rest of us'll be just fine.'

Preproduction for *Coming Up* began on November 25, 1995, with recording proper starting at the Townhouse in Goldhawk Road on December 3, two days before Neil Codling's twenty-second birthday. With Christmas approaching, Neil asked Richard if he could borrow his drum machine and four-track recorder, and, once these had been handed over, he began demoing a song called 'Tiswas'.

Brett tells me that 'Neil has been such a huge influence on the Suede sound over the years. His skill and dedication enabled us to go places we would never be able if we stuck strictly to the guitar-based format.' The comment is surely directed towards masterful Codling-penned compositions such as 'Starcrazy', and Mat Osman explains that around the time this song was written, Neil had the habit of going on fasts for twenty days or living on brown rice for two weeks. 'One evening he left looking pale, and the next day he came back with this.' This was 'Tiswas'—or, rather, the song we would one day learn to know and love as 'Starcrazy'. Brett recalls the song's origins even more vividly. 'One day Neil turned up with a wonderfully sticky little guitar piece which screamed with the violence and energy of youth.' Neil remembers the encounter as being somewhat significant: it heralded the point where he felt less of a keyboard add-on and more of a fully signed-up member of the band.

Ed Buller wasn't really sure how Neil fitted into the whole Suede picture until he heard 'Starcrazy' and someone from the band said, 'Neil wrote this one.' 'On the previous record,' he tells me, 'no one was allowed in the studio, but by this time, the recording process had become like a club. And that's why Neil got more involved.' Ed also reveals that the first time he heard the song he loved it, but he went off it quite quickly as it started to sound like a construct. 'Neil has a very scientific way of writing songs, and everything has to be just right and done at his own pace,' he suggests. 'He deals with the chaos of the universe by being disciplined in his approach to dealing with it.'

Which, when you think about it, is a strange thing to think about when you think about 'Starcrazy', as it seems so uninhibited and, ahem, *crazy*.

Richard Oakes confirms that 'Starcrazy' first came to his attention via Neil's home demo, 'Tiswas', 'in either January or February 1996,' and 'my guess is that it was after the Hanover Grand gig on January 27, so we'll say February!' Realising that it's a loaded question, and not a subject he is usually prompted to think about, I ask Richard how he felt about Neil joining the band.

'I didn't know he was going to start writing, and neither did Brett, I think,' he says, 'but it didn't really come as a surprise as I already knew he was a songwriter. Neil had played his own

160

songs at gatherings round at Brett's (including "Digging A Hole") and I think he was eager to make his mark. When the song was written, Brett excitedly handed round cassettes of the demo, and I think he was energised to know he had another composer on board, especially at a time when Saul and the others were on his back about not having enough singles. I remember finding the music very accomplished, thoughtful, and detailed, especially the guitars, which were a lot more jazzy, and Johnny Marr-like than the stuff I had been writing.

'I remember having a slight feeling that I'd have to up my game a bit,' he adds, with customary humility, 'but it was never a negative feeling—competition can be very healthy. I was more than happy to get my teeth into it and learn the parts note for note. It evolved slightly in the rehearsal room and studio, but the finished song is pretty faithful to Neil's original idea. Despite being musically complicated, the whole thing—that punk feel that I've mentioned before (I loved the line "*Electric shock bog brush hair*")—provided a shot in the arm for the album. Everyone was into it, and it was earmarked as a single. A good start for Neil!'

Of course, as soon as Suede found themselves deep into the heart of their tour promoting *Coming Up*, *Select* magazine—by some distance the best music magazine to have emerged in the 1990s—was accompanying them on the road as part of some kind of lifestyle choice. By the time the band appeared at the Liverpool Royal Court Theatre on November 28, 1996, the magazine could contain itself no longer. 'The star of Suede's winter campaign was

Neil Codling, the "Lizard Man" with the revolutionary "doing sod all" stage presence,' screamed the headline. Then, perhaps less screamingly, the article—courtesy of Andrew Male—progressed with, 'Neil Codling looks bored. So far he's smoked half a packet of fags, sorted out the contents of his trouser pockets and devoted a considerable amount of time to just running a hand through his 70s meta-public-school mop and staring off into middle space.' Later in the same article, Male was forced to concede that 'it may be nearly halfway into Suede's performance at the Royal Court, the whole venue might be rattling down to its post war foundations and Brett Anderson may well appear at the point of physical collapse but Neil Codling, Neil Codling doesn't even appear to have touched his keyboard yet. In short, he looks like a complete star.'

Naturally, I'm telling you all this because I want you to know how Neil *made a difference*. Indeed, at the risk of sounding like someone who sleeps on a pile of *Select* magazines by way of a makeshift mattress, I draw your attention to the magazine's more salient judgments on Neil's contribution to proceedings: *Select* went on to hail *Coming Up* as one of the outright albums of the year, but Suede were still the band who, since the departure of Bernard Butler, had spent 'two awkward years in a wilderness of "difficult" tours, endless drug accusations and "gayanimalsex" T-shirts—a band with little real sense of unity and a dwindling fanbase'. You could be forgiven for thinking the magazine was abandoning the cause altogether, until demureness ensued: 'Those who had witnessed January 1996's fan club show at London's Hanover Grand and the later October dates at Kilburn National knew that something had changed. It was evident in Richard Oakes's newfound assurance, in the band's choice of a Bernard-free song set and in the barely concealed violence of Brett's performance. But, most of all, it was visible in the presence of the reptilianly handsome fellow on keyboards and backing vocals—the one who appeared to do nothing at all, very well indeed.' Later, much later, one of the 'beatific Mersey teens' present at the Liverpool show enquired of our intrepid reporter, 'Do you know Neil Codling? Is he a mysterious man?' And then, her pal, equally in awe: 'Neil Codling. Very handsome.'

'Starcrazy' is a 'good stomp and has some nice guitar parts by Richard', says Saul Galpern, 'but it's probably my least favourite song on the album. I am sure I recall Ed and Brett thinking it was a single, but it's very old Suede from a Brett vocal point of view, and it's a bit too Suede-y for its own good; almost like a caricature.' Having said as much, after 'She' and 'Beautiful Ones'—two songs that appear to be all verse, or perhaps all chorus—it's satisfying to report that 'Starcrazy' is none of the above. Kicking off with a mischievous verbal nod—'*Hi*'—either to an absent friend or to a million and a half listeners, Brett somehow manages to yell '*She's star starcrazy*' like it's the most normal thing in the world, despite the fact that there's a right old racket going on behind him. Hereafter, we get some heavily emotive phraseology—'*electric shock bog brush hair*' and '*a heavy metal stutter that brains me*' being the most noteworthy examples—indicating a certain amount of incumbent stress before a more intriguing pattern begins to emerge.

'"She" is some sort of covert criticism of those who undervalue others just because they have different passions,' says Brett. '"Starcrazy" is a song about the absolute, almost quasi-religious power of pop music. It's a celebration of those moments that anyone over a certain age has felt screaming along to their favourite record in their bedrooms. I feel this *she* is a different one from the *she* in "She"—if that makes sense!—probably younger and more callow but still purposeful and dynamic and certainly not the *silly little girl* that music snobs will often portray teenage pop fans as.'

Of course, if you return to the scene of the crime—by which I mean to say, if you ask Neil what he was up to when he wrote 'Starcrazy'—he says, 'To be boring/technical, I knew that Suede's big choruses often had chord progressions that had two changes per bar ("Metal Mickey", "Animal Nitrate", "Stay Together"), which creates a forward momentum and a good backing for Brett's more soaring melodies. So I wrote the chorus chords for "Starcrazy" in a similar fashion, fleshed it out with an unnecessarily fiddly guitar part, and then did the same for the verse and the middle-eight. There was also a bridge between the verse and chorus, but Brett disregarded that, so it went no further than the demo. I used a shorter version of the middle-eight as an introduction. I programmed the drums, recorded them to cassette, played the bass, added the guitars, and mixed it. I handed the cassette to Brett with the chords so he could play along on the guitar if he wanted to play along or change a chord here or there. I had no paper to write the chords down on, so I wrote them on the back of a sign saying *Haringey Council: DUMPING STRICTLY PROHIBITED* that I'd torn off a lamppost in the street outside.'

I very much doubt whether anyone reading Neil's comments outlined above will have come to the conclusion that he could have contrived 'Starcrazy' as a kind of calling card marked *For The Attention Of Suede And All Who Sail In Her*. Nonetheless, that's an intriguing take on the subject of Neil's subsequent rise to the top of the Suede rankings as *Member Most Lauded Beyond His Mighty Brettness*, and I admire your temerity for thinking outside of the box. However, just as we are all starting to come to terms with our newfound level of insight, Neil confesses that, although he'd written music and songs for other bands, he didn't really know what he was doing in terms of writing for Suede or cooking up something for Brett to get his teeth into.

'It was all a bit hit-and-hope at first,' he says, 'but the confidence of youth counts for a lot. I'd come up with chord sequences for the verse, chorus and middle-eight that might suggest melodies for guitar parts and vocal melodies, then flesh them out with guitar lines, a bass part and a rhythm backing. I had a working knowledge of the harmonic structure and twists and turns of early Suede songs, and tried to channel those techniques and that spirit, but also putting something of myself in there, though what that is I'm not entirely sure. I had no idea what made for a great Suede song, but I had some idea of what Suede songs consisted of. I had a second-hand Satellite Les Paul copy guitar that I'd bought from a junk shop in Warwick. The proprietor smoked in the shop, and the guitar stank of cigars for years afterwards. I had no effects pedals apart from a Zoom 3030 digital multi-effects unit, which made the sticky, fizzy sound on the "Starcrazy" demo (a sound which Brett wanted to recreate on the record but which drove Ed nuts because there was no amplifier in the chain to soften the fizz). I also had a cheap Marlin Slammer bass guitar from when I'd been in bands at college. I borrowed an Alesis SR-16 drum machine and a four-track cassette recorder off the band and used those to record the demos for *Coming Up*-era songs. It was all a bit cobbled-together, but the technology available to write at home wasn't up to the standards of today, when you can approximate a studio and a backing band in a single laptop. Back then you could only do sketches of songs at home, and I had no idea what demos were supposed to sound like, so what I had was enough. If I sat on my bed in Crouch End, I could stretch out my hands and touch both walls, so I recorded in our kitchen, which was hardly any bigger.'

There's a rehearsal tape from early in 1996 that has Brett singing a different chorus in 'Starcrazy', which neither Richard nor Neil can remember doing. 'To my mind, the song arrived all in one go,' Neil tells me. 'It was an exciting moment to get the tape off Brett and hear what he'd written. It's an odd alchemy when you hand over a backing track and a fully fledged song comes back in return. We knew it was good enough for the album and that it'd fit well so there was a great energy around it. Also, it was the first thing I'd written for the band so there was an element of beginner's luck/ scoring on your debut about it.'

I ask Neil if him writing a song—and particularly a song like 'Starcrazy'—meant that he contributed lyrically. He shakes his head. 'Brett had to stand in front of people and sing these songs,' he says, 'so the rest of the band just let him get on with the lyrics. The chorus lyric seemed to me like a brash retake on "Another Brick In The Wall (Part 2)" but with a poppier tune. When I wrote the guitar part, I was imagining a more classic Suede guitar sound, but partly because of the way I'd written it (it was very fiddly) and the way it was recorded (using spiky Fender guitars rather than the rich, bluesy sound of the Gibson semi-acoustic prevalent on the first two albums), it turned out more post-punk than I'd imagined. If I were recording it now, I'd shepherd it more and try to match the sound in my head, but at the time I thought that as Ed was the producer, he'd know better than me. It was my first attempt at songwriting, after all.'

As to those lyrics, well: on 'She', Brett managed to smuggle '*No stimulation in this privatisation*' past the Syntax Police—of which I am an honorary member—without eliciting further comment, but 'Starcrazy' is a step into the unknown: the lines about education and imagination could be perfectly legitimate comments on the state of Britain's school system today, if it wasn't for the fact that

167

Brett may have finally succumbed to the Sex Pistols school of affectation. By which I mean to say . . . *affec-tache-e-own*.

Of course, Oasis had been doing this for years, and 'Cigarettes And Alcohol' (*'Is it my im-ag-in-ay-she-on?'*) and 'Some Might Say' (*'In need of ed-u-cay-shun'*) are up there with the Pistols' 'Liar' (*'You're in sus-pen-shun'*), 'Bodies' (*'She just had an a-bor-shun'*), and 'Submission' (I'm sure you're getting the picture by now) as fine examples of the *shun* genre, but you can bet Brett's never going to take any pointers from anyone other than Johnny Rotten when it comes to hand-me-downs. It's common knowledge that Brett is a long-time Pistols aficionado—as soon as Ed and I discuss the inherent truth of this suggestion, Ed is adamant that Brett has inherited some of Rotten's twang, albeit with the proviso that the latter's vocal delivery is the most unusual he has heard in the last fifty years—but, if you'll hear me out, I think there's something else going on here.

Back in 1994, when Bernard Butler walked out on Suede— or when they all walked out on each other—and Oasis and Blur first began to dictate the natural order of events, I noticed a distinct shift in Brett's onstage demeanour, and one I can only put down to several contributory factors. Bernard's leaving was bad enough in itself—perhaps it meant that Brett's inexorable rise to the top of the rock'n'roll tree was now cut off at the root— but the not-so-gently persuasive nature of this nation's noxious lad culture, engendered by the likes of Liam and Damon (admittedly, Damon's was of the more Walt Disney variety) had left its mark; gone was the louche demeanour and fluid sexuality you'd associate with the finest lyricist of his generation, to be replaced by a more brash, less complicated live version of himself, streamlined to shouting 'Aw-right' between songs and even several bouts of pogoing during some of the more frantically realised numbers. Brett got away with this, I thought at the time, by, well, remaining the finest lyricist of his generation, and I could forgive him anything—even for thinking that an abstract form of genderfluidity never got the washing up done, or helped you sell over a million records. The transformation into Brett Mk II to coincide with Suede Mk II was purely a live phenomenon, but I can't rule out the prospect that the last remnants of its existence didn't resurface on *Coming Up*, and particularly on songs like 'She' and 'Starcrazy'.

Funnily enough, when Brett turned up for his first proper press interview to accompany *Coming Up*, Roger Morton of *Vox* magazine began his piece like this:

> Four years of watching him swish like a feather boa through the melodrama of an histrionic pop existence and the first words Brett Anderson says in the flesh are: 'Oh 'ello, I'll be with you in a minute.' Four years of gender-larking, Byronic-posturing, apocalyptic fretting, drug-guzzling, arse-slapping, scrapping, bitching and trilling gorgeously and the first words are not 'Daaaaahling', or 'Sweeeetie' or even 'Delighted', just 'Oh, 'ello, I'll be with you in a

minute.' Like the sodding dentist. Or some bloke in a chip shop. Oh, well, you can get people wrong.

Later in the same article, Morton remarks, 'The twenty-eight-year-old who bustles around the smart W1 offices of his record label, Nude, is definitely a bloke. Nothing about him screams. The airs and graces are limited to the modulated Kenneth-Williams-from-the-chip-shop cadence of his speaking voice.' If you can forgive Morton his sarcastic tone, then perhaps he and I are touching on the same subject.

It's a crazy situation, all right, although I have to admit one of my favourite moments on the record is when Brett screams '*violence*' with a hint of gentle malevolence that should be envied both for its eccentricity and audacity in equal measure. The *Telegraph* newspaper commented at the time that the 'solitary trace of complete madness on the whole album comes in "Starcrazy" when, amidst a swamp of Moogs, Brett momentarily loses his marbles and hilariously hollers "violence!" for no apparent reason, but even that's come and gone in a nano-second'.

Whilst acknowledging the astuteness of this observation, you should know that me and my friends who 'worked' at Savage & Best back in the 1990s used to shout '*violence*' at one another—for no apparent reason—as and when the moment seemed most appropriate. When I tell Brett about these strange activities, he says, 'I love that story and I'm fondly picturing the scene in the office.' Luckily for all of us, he goes on to explain how the seemingly arbitrary utterance came about: 'I remember writing the song to Neil's brilliant, twisty, gnarly demo and being gripped with a madness one night and dancing around the lounge in mine and Alan's flat, smashing wine bottles against the wall and screaming *Violence!* It probably sounds crazy and deranged out of context but there's a euphoria to writing a song that is unlike anything else. It's a drug that has kept me hooked for four decades now and shows no signs of loosening its grip.'

I'm glad we've cleared that up, although there's something else I need to get off my chest:

'*Violence.*'

13

CURIOUSER AND CURIOUSER

&&I decided to do some research—not
something I'd recommend for anyone over the
age of eighteen—and discovered that LSD
didn't exist when Lewis Carroll wrote *Alice In
Wonderland*. All right, I admit it, I knew that
already, and *research* is stretching it a bit . . . &&

*'If it's a single, it'll be called "Lovely Day". If it's
not a single, I'll think of something clever.'*

If there's one song you could imagine being part of the *Dog
Man Star* repertoire, it's 'Picnic By The Motorway'. Originally
hailed as an item of interest called 'Lovely Day', 'PBTM' is an
urban love song based, according to Mat Osman, 'on a melody
that sounds like an Asda advert.' Mat acknowledges the song as
having a taste of 'that British pastoral psychedelic thing to it—
Floyd and Robert Wyatt and all that', and Richard having 'such
a knowledge of weird proggy British stuff like Caravan'. Having
said that, it's entirely possible that 'PBTM' may be just 'a druggy-
sounding song about getting off your head', and, perhaps, the
only track on the album where you could close your eyes and
think, *Is this Bernard Butler on guitar?* Appropriately enough, it
was the first thing that Brett and Richard wrote together after
Bernard's departure.

Richard confirms that he wrote 'PBTM' in late 1994—film
director Mike Christie remembers him writing the song at his
house in Mile End, when Richard was lodging with him on the first
stages of the *Dog Man Star* tour—and that it is his favourite song
on *Coming Up*. 'It was just an experiment really, learning how to
operate a four-track,' Richard says. 'It was very soft and dreamy at
first. We weren't trying to write an album at that point, so it didn't
have a context or have to fit into a sonic template. It must have
been some point in '95 when Brett wrote the song around it, and

it was always going to be on the A-list for the album. Making it fit into the *Coming Up* universe meant having to evolve it a bit. The choruses are a lot brighter and harsher than they were originally.'

Brighter and harsher? That's some kind of take on it.

Ed Buller talks about a palette of sounds that are unique to every band you work with, and Suede's palette having been established with 'The Drowners'. 'Richard was very good at mimicking Bernard at first,' he says now. 'His playing was superb, and in some ways better than Bernard's. He could play the same every day and was always on it, but he needed to develop his own sound.' When I mention Ed's comments to Richard, he tells me that 'PBTM' 'features a lot of fairly heavy guitars and wiry, bendy lead sounds that were sort of trademark sounds, used on other songs. And it's true to say there was a palette of sounds, but it was created by Ed. I didn't know enough about the studio at that point and was happy to just sit and play, while Ed and Gary Stout fiddled with various effects and toys.'*

The band actually thought about placing the sound effects at the start of the song, recorded using binaural recording techniques, so that if you were listening on headphones, it would feel like the cars were driving through your head to make it even more trippy.

---

* In the early to mid 90s, Buller and Stout—together with fellow producers Flood and Dave Bessell—actually formed a freeform electronic retro-pioneer supergroup called Node. Appropriately enough, in electronic terms, a node is a point of zero current or voltage, whilst, in general terms, it is a point of intersection, a junction. Presumably this, and the fact that all four of them were obsessed with analogue technology, explains why they hit on the name in the first place.

Ed recalls the band wanting to record some 'real motorway effects' but can't remember ever going to a motorway to bring about such authentic eccentricities. I ask him whether the band might have used a BBC *Sound Effects* sample instead, and Ed agrees, before suggesting that Gary may have taken it upon himself to record 'real motorway sounds' without his knowledge.

'Picnic By The Motorway' was pretty much set in stone by the time Neil came along. Richard had originally written a piano part for the demo and, although Neil played piano on a very early version of the song—there's some lovely footage of this event on YouTube—Ed didn't like it, so it was ditched. Neil did play piano on the song's live excursions for a while, but ended up switching to acoustic guitar, 'except for the middle-eight, which has a Mellotron—a keyboard that's a kind of tape-based proto-sampler—on it'. He suggests that this helped give the song a trippy vibe, and, at the time, they were aiming for something like the second half of T. Rex's song 'Tenement Lady'. 'The way the chords of "Picnic" loop round is quite odd,' he says. 'It's definitely not a standard rock or pop chord progression, and that adds to the otherworldly vibe. The song's arrangement is a reflection and an amplification of that oddness. There are 60s rock staples (fuzzy guitar, Hammond organ, and Mellotron strings) mixed with a 90s trippy jangle.'

'Picnic By The Motorway' is effectively two songs: the 'Asda advert', where Brett innocently promotes the merits of it being '*such a lovely day*', together with the multi-layered, multi-faceted

175

'trippy' section, where you're not quite sure what's going on. Inevitably, both songs often merge from a two-lane highway into a narrow one-lane stretch, creating a confusing kaleidoscopic hinterland betwixt daydream and reality.

Enamoured with such insight, I tell Ed that the song is possibly the strangest Suede song I have ever heard. 'Well,' he says, 'the guitar is heavily processed and put through a wah-wah pedal and into a Leslie [speaker]. It's a great, weird mix with a slight clash of keys which are slightly out of tune and occasionally clash with the vocal. There's a whammy bar and a bender and lots of vocal effects. And when "*day*" lands on the bend, it's a very guitar hero moment.'

There are several not-so-hidden drug references on 'PBTM', so you can be pretty sure all is not as it seems. The opening line, '*I'm so sorry to hear about the news*', is delivered with such casual insouciance, one can only conclude that Brett is not even trying to hit the right note. Perhaps he's not bothered whether he sounds out of it, but that's surely the point: it's real, it's trippy, and it's pure Syd Barrett. Right back in the early days, I'd detected a connection between Brett and Barrett, and that opening line appears 'innocent' enough to be worthy of Barrett himself. Of course, having said that, it's swathed in such huge amounts of reverb that you can't help thinking you're immersed in the midst of a dense fog of some kind. Herein, we can't be entirely sure that this '*fog*' hasn't caused the '*speeding disaster*' we encounter in the second verse, but at least a bottle of something or other arrives just in time to offer us a drink/drug-induced way out.

I don't want you to think that LSD is involved in proceedings in any way at all, but at the end of the first verse, Brett mutters, really quite urgently, '*There's a gap in the fence down by the nature reserve*', and we're instantly transported to somewhere rather splendid, the languid, semi-hallucinogenic borders of the verse now abandoned for the sunny uplands of '*a lovely day*'. The '*gap in the fence*' is, of course, a rabbit hole of sorts, and suitably charged with as much metaphorical significance as the one in *Alice In Wonderland*. And just as that rabbit hole is a place where everything begins, symbolising a gateway into a new world, so we are catapulted into…what? It's almost as if the rabbit hole has been turned on its head, and the new world we now find ourselves in is not remotely new at all, instead perhaps just the most perfect version of reality we could ever imagine.

Or, in other words:

SUCH A LOVELY DAY.

* * *

I decided to do some research—not something I'd recommend for anyone over the age of eighteen—and discovered that LSD didn't exist when Lewis Carroll wrote *Alice In Wonderland*. All right, I admit it, I knew that already, and 'research' is stretching it a bit as I actually just looked on the National Institute On Drug Abuse For Teens website, where I was told that 'Lewis Carroll's writing is much too imaginative and clever to be done by someone on drugs'. Naturally, this is a hilarious conclusion for all sorts of reasons—

not least of which is the fact that the book you are reading is imaginative and clever, and quite clearly written on drugs—but despite the fact that LSD almost certainly did exist when Brett Anderson wrote 'Picnic By The Motorway', I don't think the song is particularly about an acid trip either: it's well documented that Brett used to take industrial quantities of cocaine, crack, and heroin in the 1990s, but he also waved his creative wand in the general direction of a sizeable amount of ecstasy, and I'm pretty sure *'Just put on your trainers and get out of it with me'*—a line used at the end of the second verse at a similar juncture as the *'gap in the fence'* at the end of the first verse—is nailed on as an invitation to dress one's trotters in leisure footwear and partake of several Scooby Snacks, preferably both at the same time.

'Picnic By The Motorway' has been called out as 'the terrifying mirror image of *Coming Up*'s pop songs', as well as 'a stupid, squalid sally into the outside world despatched with all the elan of a suicide note'. I am guessing that these comments are meant as some kind of caustic criticisms, but they only serve to remind me of the suggestion I made earlier—that 'Picnic By The Motorway' is the most *Dog Man Star*-esque track on *Coming Up*. It makes perfect sense, therefore, that 'PBTM' is also the druggiest song hereabouts. (*Druggiest* is not a real word, but I think we know each other well enough by now for me to be able to get away with such frippery.) *Dog Man Star* is riddled with references to ecstasy; when the lead track, 'Introducing The Band', kicks off with *'Dog man star took a suck on a pill'*, it really is a bit of a heads up, E-wise.

Admittedly, '*smack cracks at your window*' in 'We Are The Pigs' might be something of an in-joke, but 'The Asphalt World' is so full of disco-biscuit chutzpah, you may as well have half now and half later. '*She comes to me / I supply her with ecstasy,*' caws Brett, and it still sounds more sweaty and fucked-up than the innocent affectations offered up in 'Beautiful Ones'.

* * *

Those of you who are paying attention may have twigged that I lost it (to Bostik, yeah) in the section above. However, in defence of this narrative, I would like to propose that the '*gap in the fence*' I identified as a metaphorical link to a higher state of being may have clouded my judgment and somehow catapulted me into another dimension. Which leads me to suggest that this is as good a moment as any to reflect on *The Drug Question*.

Throughout the 1990s, Brett was constantly quizzed on his own drug usage, as well as recreational drugs in general, and how his lyrics might represent the realities of his lifestyle. During the lifetime of the *Coming Up* press campaign—broadly stretching from August '96 on the eve of the album's release to the release of the 'Filmstar' single in August the following year—these inquisitions reached pandemic proportions. You could have forgiven Brett for being somewhat of a curmudgeon at this point in proceedings—perhaps confessing to all sorts of terribly dangerous, narcotic activity involving the Queen, her Corgis, and several of her nearest and dearest—but he handled all enquiries with the kind of charm and efficiency we've come to expect from someone of such elegant character.

In January 1997, Brett was asked whether he was 'strictly speaking, in the opium poet tradition from Coleridge and Blake through to Morrison and Bowie?' 'No,' he replied, 'people keep saying, *Oh, he uses drugs to write songs*, but it isn't like that. I take drugs for purely recreational reasons because I really enjoy them. What's the film with Elizabeth Taylor? *Cat On A Hot Tin Roof*? Where Paul Newman's trying to explain why he's an alcoholic: it flicks a switch, your brain just turns off. And that's why I take drugs, because I'm thinking all the time. Otherwise, I need to let off steam. The one bastion of evilness in the drugs world is heroin. I know coke and E have got evil connotations, but only in the tabloid press. Anyone who's got half a brain sees through all that. The whole ecstasy panic really wound me up. All this misinformation and all these people in suburbia who've never touched a drug in their lives believing it all. But the papers are allowed to tell these absolute lies because it's for some *moral crusade* to stop people killing themselves.'

Naturally, Brett's revelations about his ongoing drug proclivities were cleverly barbed directives of the highest order, and not to be sniffed at. How else are you meant to deal with the received wisdom of some of the more ill-informed sections of the anti-drug community? Well, dismiss oneself as being both boring and ill-advised, for starters! From here on in, you are now no doubt expecting me to tell you that I think 'Picnic By The Motorway' is just about the most casually realised evocation of a time and place one could ever imagine, and I am not here to disappoint.

When I first heard 'PBTM', I loved the way it made you feel that Bowie had accidentally stumbled across an early incarnation of Pink Floyd and decided to join them, just for the hell of it. Richard's superbly meandering guitar work does its best to maintain the illusion, and I am assured that if you actually take a mind-altering drug before listening to the song, you are quite likely to conclude that the Bowie/Floyd hybrid I had originally thought of as part of a personal crusade to change the world's conception of reality is actually very much of a reality check, ahem, reality-wise.

'Picnic By The Motorway' turns out to be Richard's favourite song on the album. 'I love how it starts as a distant strummed acoustic, gradually builds and goes on a journey, and the end is a trippy, neon rush of weird sounds and weird riffs,' he says, before confirming that 'it was called "Lovely Day" right up until the eleventh hour. In fact, I can remember seeing a mock-up of the album artwork with *Lovely Day* as the title—it was only when I saw the finished CD that I learned its actual title.'

Later, when I pluck up the courage to ask Brett why 'Picnic By The Motorway' is so fucking *out there*, he kind of agrees. 'Yes, it's an odd, trippy sort of thing, isn't it,' he says, 'but still with its feet planted firmly in pop land. It's one of the more narrative things I've written, very much a story of two souls wandering together near the hard shoulders looking at the traffic. I've always been obsessed by motorways and concrete and the furniture of the edge-lands. There's a brilliant book by J.G. Ballard called *Concrete Island* where a man gets trapped in a motorway central reservation and has to live there eking out an existence in one of those forgotten, functional, manmade places. I find there's so much poetry and melancholy there—these places where people never really settle or stop or even properly look at. There's also a fascinating seediness—the torn up pornographic magazines, the fumbling lovers sat in parked cars. Places where people go to do something illicit.'

I've often wondered whether 'Picnic By The Motorway' should be seen as some kind of companion piece to 'Daddy's Speeding' off *Dog Man Star*. What I mean to say is that both tracks don't quite fit in within the constraints of their surroundings, and whilst *Dog Man Star* is complicated enough to be blessed with having no constraints at all, 'Daddy's Speeding' is so out of keeping with anything else on that record that it must have a friend somewhere else amongst Suede's repertoire. Indeed, both songs employ reverb to such an extent that they must be trying to say something out of the ordinary, and we know from previous correspondence that they both use driving/car terminology. 'Daddy's Speeding' is reportedly a song that centres around the actor James Dean and the crash that took his life, although it's also been accused of containing several references to *Crash*, another J.G. Ballard tome that Brett has cited as an influence on his work. But 'Picnic By The Motorway'? It has the same vibe, doesn't it? By which I mean to say, we are in a time and space where we don't quite know what we're meant to think.

Oh, and about that gap in the fence? I was worried that I was making things up just to amuse myself, so I asked Brett if he could shed some light on the matter. Naturally, he was as charming as ever, claiming that, when he was a kid, he 'used to live next to a dump which in later years became a nature reserve so yes, the lyric was very much inspired by experience but, of course like all art, it embroiders that a little'.

So there was a gap in the fence. I knew it, I fucking knew it.

14

SHINY HAPPY PEOPLE

"If you really want to know about my *inner world* then we should pursue our relationship elsewhere, but it involves a chemistry lesson back at a school I never attended, together with several classmates I never met, and a chemical high we never got to share. Until, that is, the moment I heard this song."

'I've taken drugs in the past—but anyone who thinks that by dropping a tab of acid they are going to write "Strawberry Fields Forever" has got another think coming.'

'The Chemistry Between Us' is often referred to as the anchor song on *Coming Up*, but this is patently untrue: unlike 'The Asphalt World', undoubtedly the key song to tune in and drop out to on *Dog Man Star*, 'The Chemistry Between Us' is far too long—at seven minutes—to be anything other than an indulgence, or at best, a curious anomaly, on an album with card-carrying aspirations towards pure pop perfection.

When *Coming Up* finally saw the light of day, 'The Chemistry Between Us' immediately became something of a talking point. No doubt this was due to the fact that it heralded the arrival of Neil Codling as a songwriting force, but the song also saw Richard Oakes finally turning up as guitarist with a style that he could claim as his own: it features some of his most luxurious and melodic riffery, and provides a perfectly balanced backdrop to the 50s retro-glam of the chaos that surrounds it, as well as Brett's cute Judy Garland *la-la-la* laments.

Neil reveals that the origins of 'Chemistry' came from a chord progression he occasionally strummed on guitar in the studio in late 1995. 'It had a nagging chromatic three-chord descent that was reminiscent of "Do You Want To Know A Secret",' he tells me. 'I recorded it in a very rudimentary fashion on cassette and called it "GBH" so as not to forget it and promptly forgot about it. On the other side of the tape I ended up recording a demo called "Buckley", which eventually turned into a Suede song called "Simon". I thought Brett would like "Buckley", so I gave him the cassette. Brett didn't listen to "Buckley" and, instead, rewound it to the side with "GBH" on it and wrote "The Chemistry Between Us" to it.

'That demo is now lost to history, but I remember the first line wasn't "*And maybe we're just kids who've grown*" but "*Nina, now you're on your own*". Even as an acoustic demo it had promise. At Mat's place on North Pole Road, where I was staying, I worked up a better demo with drum machine and bass and added the guitar riff refrain to the intro and post-chorus (under where the *la-la-las* ended up). This was the version presented to the rest of the band. I think it was the lyric more than the feel of the song that made it a good fit for the album, but its lightness of touch and length made it a fitting track to put second last.'

Mat suggests that the song uses 'an ancient chord sequence that you get in anything from "Puff The Magic Dragon" to "I Don't Like Mondays"'. He goes on to say, 'We started out with a set of rules for this album: no gratuitous reverb, no adding instruments for the sake of it. By the time we got to this one, we threw all those rules out the window.' Indeed, there are essentially two solos going on towards the end of the song, followed by two complementary riffs. Ed had tasked Neil and Richard to come up with riffs that fitted over the verse chords to close out the song: Richard came back with the overdriven melody you can hear at the end, while

186

Neil came up with the high arpeggio line. For the record, Ed thought neither of them did what he wanted, but they recorded both, and they both ended up being left on the record in lieu of anything better.

These days, the band are divided on the merits of 'Chemistry' as a contender for anything other than *Just Another Song From The Coming Up Coffers Of Excellence*. Simon, Mat, and Neil like it because it sounds Stones-y and romantic, and Ed and Brett seem to dislike it for the same reasons. According to Neil, Ed in particular thought it sounded like a needlessly extended jam, whilst Neil himself has always come down on the side of 'the dreamy nature of the meandering guitar coda, which, along with the strings, gives the song a dreamy depth at the perfect spot on the album'. For his part, Ed doesn't even think the song sounds like Suede but more like a band 'wanting to be the Rolling Stones' and even 'like a shampoo advert!'

Not long after the album was released, the band started playing 'Europe Is Our Playground' live, and Brett—apparently—began to regret including 'Chemistry' on the record instead of 'Europe'. I say *apparently* since Ed maintains that the subject was never discussed. 'I would have said, *Fuck, yeah,*' he says now—which makes me think he really hates 'Chemistry', a song he confesses that he didn't know 'how to end'. How different the record would have sounded with 'Europe' replacing 'Chemistry' is a moot point: it's not that much of a stretch to imagine *Coming Up* sans 'Chemistry' and emboldened with a song as beautifully nuanced as 'Europe', but as both songs are up there as two of my favourite Suede tunes of all time—and therefore, according to the best judge of such matters, two of the best songs of all time—I have to defer to the gods of impartiality and conclude that I cannot choose between the pair of them. Naturally, if Brett had had the foresight to herald *Coming Up* as an album that was about to spawn 'eleven hits', I wouldn't now find myself backed into a corner.

The gorgeous string arrangement that features throughout 'Chemistry' was recorded at Olympic Studios in Barnes, and although Neil maintains that Craig Armstrong was there to conduct and 'accentuate the chromaticism in the main chord progression', the band thought they sounded a little syrupy, so they got changed. However, this is only half the story, since Armstrong had actually written the *wrong* chord progression—something that only Richard seemed brave enough to point out. Neil now wonders what Craig—'a fantastic musician and a brilliant arranger'—must have thought when Richard made his way into the live room and began telling the string players to listen to him and disregard the written arrangement. Both Ed and Neil can distinctly remember, Craig 'standing there in disbelief'. And then Neil reminds me that Andrew Loog Oldham once said, 'Every boy of nineteen should have their own orchestra'—'and here was nineteen-year-old Richard living the dream'.

'"Chemistry" was very different from everything else,' says Richard now. 'It went on a journey. I think Neil says he spent a lot of time doing a whole demo of it where the verse was different, although that version resurfaced in 2000 as "Simon". On the B-side of the cassette he gave Brett was a quick, scratchy version of the basic chorus chords, and that was the thing Brett wrote to.' Richard also recalls Neil coming to his flat in early '96 and recording another demo of it 'after getting very drunk. That recording only exists on Hi-8 tape,' says Richard, 'and I'm currently having them digitised, so soon I'll be able to hear just how much of a state we were in! But the song got written and we rehearsed it and started recording it. It was a classic example of Ed insisting that we had more guitar riffs all over it, so Neil went and wrote a couple (including the intro riff), and I went and wrote a couple. It had to evolve and have a landscape, as we wanted it to be a sprawling anchor-track, not a traditional structure.'

Maybe there's something in that *anchor song* theory after all—and it's interesting to note that Brett has always had a theory about an album being like a seesaw and needing a fulcrum and some kind of anchor for it to make sense. As I suggested quite recently, I consider 'The Asphalt World' to fit the bill perfectly when it comes to *Dog Man Star*, but what we do know about 'The Chemistry Between Us' is that it's a song lamenting the emptiness of it all. It's surely also a comment on anyone who has enjoyed drugs with someone they have nothing in common with—aside from their communal drug use—although, having said that, I've often wondered how much one needs to know about any song in order to enjoy it; indeed, whether insight is some kind of benevolent tool charged with heightening pleasure, or whether it's best not to know anything about the song at all.

* * *

Back when the prospect of turning twenty was becoming something of a growing concern, I had more of an unhealthy obsession with bands and their music than I do now. R.E.M. were my icons of choice, and, after seeing the band perform live on *The Tube* on November 18, 1983—a Sex Pistols at Manchester's Lesser Free Trade Hall in June 1976 moment of awakening for me, and another event I didn't attend in person—I immediately tracked down their five-track *Chronic Town* EP (their first release for IRS in 1982) on import and debut single 'Radio Free Europe' (available on Hib-Tone the year before that). At the time, I paid more money for these items than I care to think about, but many years later—after witnessing the band's first hundred UK gigs and sleeping in my car for a good deal of them—R.E.M. released 'Shiny Happy People', a song that Michael Stipe subsequently disowned and disliked as much as I did. The track is surely one of the band's more elaborate attempts to dabble with bubblegum pop, but it was enjoyed with gay abandon by an enormous amount of the listening hordes, all of whom remained unaware that they were part of an experiment between the best band in the world—or so I thought at the time—and the rest of humanity.

The ploy backfired spectacularly, as acknowledged by *Q* magazine in 2015, when it included the song in a list of Ten

190

Terrible Records By Great Artists, and by the band themselves, who refused to play the song live pretty much throughout their entire career. In a vain attempt to demonstrate my point, I have learnt to keep my mouth shut when distant acquaintances cite 'Shiny Happy People' as their favourite R.E.M. song. Presumably these are the very same people who, in keeping with *Top Of The Pops* presenter Simon Parkin, thought 'Orange Crush' was 'great on a summer's day, mmm'—despite the song's title referring to the chemical defoliant Agent Orange used in the Vietnam War.

On September 1, 1997, the day after the death of Princess Diana, The Verve released 'The Drugs Don't Work' and it went straight to no.1. The song's enormous success was surely down to the fact that nearly everyone who bought it did so under the misapprehension that it was about the pitfalls of taking too many drugs in one sitting. Of course, the truth of the matter is that the song is about Richard Ashcroft watching his father die in hospital—a suggestion that becomes ever more likely when you consider some of the lyrics with this in mind, to wit, *'I hope you're thinking of me / As you lay down on your side'* and *'I'll sing in your ear again'*.*

---

* Richard actually wrote the song in early 1995 and performed it on The Verve's *A Northern Soul* tour later that year, and everyone at my PR/management company Savage & Best, who managed and publicised the band for their first two albums, was always under the impression that the song was about Richard's dad. Richard went on to win Songwriter Of The Year at the Ivor Novello Awards in 1998, an occasion that prompted him to comment, somewhat later, 'That song is so misunderstood. I was walking up to the stage—and really you would expect better from a serious music award such as the Ivor Novello—there were all these pictures of hypodermic needles all around the stage. Bloody irresponsible.'

And yet? And yet, who decides how anyone should enjoy a song? Do those who have a deeper understanding of a song's meaning automatically have a right to enjoyment in its purest form? Richard eventually chose not to discuss 'The Drugs Don't Work' at all. 'What I've found with lyrics is sometimes people's own interpretations are on another level to mine, certainly with songs like "The Drugs Don't Work",' he told *Songfacts* in 2018. 'I realised twenty years ago, if I underline with a big marker pen, *The Drugs Don't Work equals whatever*, then I'm killing it for people.'

Ed Buller throws his hat into the ring by suggesting that 'the business of controlling an idea ends when you release the idea', which makes perfect sense. Or, if you will, songs, once they are written, have no need of their writers. So, let's not even get started on The Police and 'Every Breath You Take'. Or indeed Suede's 'Heroine', a track that confused the hell out of my mother for several years.*

---

* Anyone who has read my first book will be aware that conversations with my mother often wandered into the realms of the surreal. For instance, after hearing The Fall's 'Repetition'—'*All you daughters and sons / Who are sick of fancy music / We dig repetition*'—she once asked me if the band were deconstructing music *in order for us to reassess it,* and then, in what seemed like the same breath, suggested that The Jesus & Mary Chain had ceased to exist the minute they learned how to control their feedback and audiences had stopped rioting at their gigs. Naturally, she was right on both counts, but she didn't have everything her own way.

'Mum, I love "Golden Brown" by the Stranglers. Do you like it as much as I do?' I would ask her.

'Yes,' she'd reply.

'Aha,' I'd counter. 'It's about heroin.'

And then.

'What about "Perfect Day" by Lou Reed? Would you like to hear that?'

Naturally, I digress—it's part of the job description—but the reason I am telling you all this is that 'The Chemistry Between Us' is far and away my favourite song on *Coming Up*, and perhaps even one of my favourite songs of all time. Brett disagrees. In fact, when I tell him this, he says, 'At the risk of coming across as arsy, it's easily my least favourite track on the record. But *vive la différence*, as they say. Personally, I just wish we'd included "Europe Is Our Playground" instead of this, but agreeing to disagree is fine, and it's lovely that people have fondness for things which sometimes I'm indifferent to. I find the music a little MOR and tame, to be honest. There was this lovely YouTube video of two girls from Indonesia or somewhere playing the song on their acoustic guitars in their bedroom, and that performance moved me much more that the slightly over-polished version on *Coming Up*.'

Richard is adamant that 'Chemistry' differs from 'Starcrazy'—

'Ooh yes, I like that.'

Sorry, Mum, that's about heroin too!'

And then again.

'I know you like "There She Goes" by The Las's. Shall we play that?'

'Yes, please!'

'Heroin again, Mum, sorry.'

And. Finally.

'Mum, I'm not going to mess about anymore. Can we listen to "Heroine" by Suede?'

'I'm not falling for that again,' she'd say. 'I know for a fact that's about heroin!'

'Well, that's where you're wrong,' I'd announce with a flourish, 'because it's actually spelt with an e on the end, and it's about female idols and empowerment.'

At this point my mother would sigh, the faintest of smiles on her lips, suggesting that she was on to my little game.

at the time, we are discussing the subject of both songs emanating from the pen of Neil Codling—to the extent that 'there was room for build-ups and breakdowns and the band making it breathe. I remember it being much more of a group effort. It became obvious that it would benefit from having strings on it, so we got Craig Armstrong to compose an arrangement along with "She".'

Suede didn't play 'The Chemistry Between Us' live all that much; in fact, it wasn't until February 15, 1997—after fifty gigs in four months—that they played it all. That night, at King George's in Blackburn (a performance that marked the first time the band played the album live in its entirety and included Brett duetting with support act Raissa on 'Green As Sea'), Neil Codling commented that he 'really liked playing it because I got to play the guitar on it'. Neil's gentle reflections that evening surely demonstrate the importance of the song to him as a developing songwriter, as well as his newly acquired status as an integral member of Suede, both live and on record. The studio version of the song features him playing keyboards with 'a fairground organ feel in the verse', and he remembers 'scrabbling on the floor of Master Rock playing the bass pedals on a Hammond C3 organ while Richard doubled the part on the lower manual. I played some guitar on it too—some bits towards the end, and a tremolo part in the bridges—but I don't recall how much of it made the final mix. Ed was happy to have me play guitar back then, but ever since, Richard does pretty much all the guitars.

'It's a shame "Chemistry" doesn't get more live outings,' he says, 'as the fans love it and it's always fun to play, but as it's a vibe piece, it's difficult to fit into the classic energy flow of a setlist. But it works perfectly on the album and takes it on a journey of euphoria and de-focus before we get to the simple, home-straight feel of "Saturday Night".'*

* * *

The key lyrical couplet on 'Chemistry' is '*Class A, Class B / Is that the only chemistry between us?*'—Ed Buller is adamant that he didn't like the song until Brett came in with the melody and the lyric that sustains it—a keenly signposted comment directed towards social class and the vacuity of drug use amongst the spiritually unconnected. Even so, I must confess that I have always enjoyed this song at its crudest level, as a visceral experience that is surely in contrast to what the song is really about. Indeed, to be honest for a moment—there's a time and place for everything—the first time I heard 'The Chemistry Between Us', I had a sense of its meaning but immediately became immersed in an inner world of my own making.†

---

* Richard also recalls Armstrong doing an arrangement for 'Beautiful Ones' that exists on sheet music but was never recorded.

† Of course, if you really want to know about my 'inner world' then we should pursue our relationship elsewhere, but it involves a chemistry lesson back at a school I never attended, together with several classmates I never met, and a chemical high we never got to share. Until, that is, the moment I heard this song. Yes, that's right, I heard this song with someone I apparently had nothing in common with other than our shared drug intake. And we took drugs together. Is that a criminal offence?

195

Richard tells me that he never really focussed too much on the lyrics of 'Chemistry', but 'they work very well as a statement of where Brett's life was at the time (fast forward two years and ditto with "Down") and the fans love the sentiment'.

Having revealed as much, Brett seems happy enough that I like the '*Class A, Class B*' line. 'Thank you,' he says. 'It seems to neatly sum up the emptiness lurking behind most hedonism.' I am happy to tell you that I'm happy he's happy—we could be here for hours—but I still maintain that the song is a *Great Escape* for me—please understand that I am referring to the film starring Steve McQueen rather than the Blur album of the same name—and perhaps that's what Suede have always meant to me: they are my best means of escape from the humdrum and the everyday, even if they do write songs about the humdrum and the everyday as if our lives depended on it.

We have been here before: Suede are nothing if not the masters of the art of smuggling the ugly vagaries of reality past the Truth Police, and don't we just know it; 'Animal Nitrate' managed to get a not-so-thinly disguised reference to a drug associated with sex and the gay community on to *Top Of The Pops* and the BRIT Awards; 'So Young' appeared to condone the use of heroin but then headed off any critics at the pass with a last-minute suggestion to '*chase the dragon from our homes*'; and I've lost count of the amount of times their songs hide in plain sight amidst the banality of their surroundings. 'The Chemistry Between Us' is something of a misnomer in this regard, as it appears to do exactly what it says on

196

the tin. However, it's still one of the finest examples of the type of 1990s kitchen-sink drama the band are associated with; the song's sanguine reflections on being young and easily led—and perhaps not even tired of it—inevitably lead to the kids getting out of their heads, and everything is delivered with such gay abandon, it's worthy of a Pinter play.

To conclude our discussions, Ed Buller throws his hat into the ring with the suggestion that there was 'originally a bit of a "Wild Horses" vibe going on there, but that went. It has something in common with "The Wild Ones", but without the chilling feel. It's optimistic, which was the mood of the recording.'

So, it's a song that sits halfway between 'The Wild Ones' and 'Wild Horses'? I can live with that.

15

BALLAD IDEA

> **"**It's only as the song canters towards its delightful conclusion that you notice how the deceptively simple counter melody has somehow sealed the deal.
>
> And here I would like to point out that, as any pretentious art critic will tell you, there's a difference between *simple* and *deceptively simple.***"**

'This is the first Suede album you'd listen to before you went out.'

Coming Up signs off as an ever-present phenomenon in our lives with 'Saturday Night', a song that's been accused of many things and yet still survives the interrogation. The song started out as a demo called 'Ballad Idea' and is notable for the fact that, at the time, it prompted Neil Codling to suggest that *Coming Up* was 'the first Suede album you'd listen to before you went out'. The assessment seems peculiarly apposite since the song presents itself as an anomaly in the Suede canon—surely not another one, I hear you cry—and specifically as an ultra-traditional nod in the direction of a female partner who the song's protagonist is keen on placating with reference to her Saturday-night demands.

Neil offers perhaps more revelatory conclusions as to the song's merits when he tells me that 'one of the signatures of Suede songs is a bit of grit in the oyster, a twist in the chords or the melodies, a sneer or a snarl, and "Saturday Night" has none of those. It could be a straight MOR ballad. *Coming Up* was a record made by the kids smoking behind the bike sheds, but "Saturday Night" was preppy and relatively polite. Maybe it only gets a pass because of the songs that came before it on the album. For a long time, we'd end concerts with it, as it's a lighters-in-the-air, arms-around-each-other song, a moment of clarity after the messy highs of the previous nine songs.'

Richard says that 'Ballad Idea' was a very simple idea to start with. 'There was no mystery,' he tells me. 'I wrote a progressive, arpeggiated guitar piece and put it over the top of the drumbeat from "Siamese Twins" by The Cure, perhaps to give it a darker edge. But Brett wanted it to be warm, off its face, and romantic-sounding, and he didn't like the slightly darker and more uncertain original chorus I had for it, so we wrote a new one that was more in fitting with the verse. The song seemed to chime with everyone, and we demoed it at the Church. I don't recall anyone saying that it didn't sound like Suede—in fact, I only became aware of that when I read the reviews of *Coming Up*. Some people couldn't believe that the same band that produced *Dog Man Star* could present something as poppy, embracing, and soft as this. But that was the point: it wasn't the same band, and I was glad that "Saturday Night" demonstrated that to people so clearly. Having said that, I don't think we've written a song like that since. Maybe it was a one-off.'

Neil played keyboards on 'Saturday Night' as well as some overdriven Fender Rhodes in the verse and middle-eight, some 'soaring synths' in the chorus, and some brass Mellotron in the middle-eight. He did a lot of high, layered backing vocals, too—if you listen carefully, you can also hear him playing the vocal melody on the synth—but readily admits that the song was written and arranged by Richard before he joined, so he didn't need to add much. Whatever he contributed, one of the *soaring* synths that Neil is no doubt referring to is a Yamaha CS80, an analogue synthesizer popularised by Vangelis in the 70s and 80s (particularly on his 1982 *Blade Runner* soundtrack), and a 220lb behemoth of a contraption notable for having a touch-sensitive keyboard that produces lighter notes the harder you press the keys.

'Saturday Night' was the first song to be completed during the *Coming Up* sessions, and Saul Galpern in particular was made up when he heard it. 'I don't agree with any negative opinions about the song,' he says now. 'I really love it—it carries a weightiness for me in that I think it's really good songwriting with that lovely refrain at the end. Obviously, it became an anthem to end the set, but the melodies remind me of a really old crooner's song from the 50s that my dad would play on his piano. I always thought it would be the only song on the album someone could cover.'

Back in the summer of 1996, I set up a meeting between Brett and the acclaimed British author Hanif Kureishi. The fruits of their conversation appeared in the August 1996 edition of *Arena* magazine. It was not unusual for Brett to have such intellectually charged promotional duties thrust upon him as part of his everyday activities, and I vividly recall arranging photo sessions with iconic lensmen David Bailey and Gered Mankowitz, as well as a joint interview with David Bowie—the details of which some readers may have stumbled across in my first book—and yet further encounters featuring Neil Tennant and Derek Jarman. But for the purposes of our ongoing story, it is interesting to note that as part of their conversation, Brett told Kureishi, 'There's ten tracks on the new album and six of them are gonna be singles. The problem with the last album was it was a fucking good record but it was fucking difficult to sell. There were only two good singles on it and one of them went above people's heads—"The Wild Ones"—and the only good single, you know the thing about it, a good single isn't necessarily a good song. A good single is something like "Saturday Night" by Whigfield. It's one of the most boring songs ever written, but there are certain things that work on the radio.'

Perhaps, therefore, we should consider 'Saturday Night' as Suede's attempt at outmanoeuvring Whigfield—just a thought—although Brett is adamant that he finds 'Saturday Night' 'extremely moving. For me it captures something very real. I love that there's a joy to its melancholy. On *Coming Up*, I really wanted to write songs that were emotive but without being tragic so instead of the tortured sentiments of "Still Life" or "Asphalt World", I chose to document one of those simple, everyday emotions but hopefully give it a romance and a charm. I've always loved the idea that everyday life contains poetry. I love all those painters like Pieter de Hooch and Hammershoi and Millet who paint scenes of ordinariness but give them such beauty and dignity, and I wanted to try and capture a night out on the tiles with my lover in the same way.'

For the record, the lines '*Today she's been sat there / Sat there in a black chair / Office furniture*' were inspired by a Patrick Caulfield painting, and are particular favourites of Brett's, although he goes on to say the song 'was probably influenced slightly by that kind of mid-90s zeitgeist, but as *Dog Man Star* had so aggressively rejected all that it felt that we could allow ourselves a little leeway and drift towards the centre ground a little but do it on our own terms.'

When I ask Ed Buller about 'Saturday Night' and 'Lazy' being the two songs that considered opinion has down as the most throwaway offerings on the album, he says, 'The thing is, when Brett comes up with songs like this, everyone just asks him where the hidden meaning of the song is and where the bodies are buried. It must be frustrating for him.' Ed's thoughts on the issue are confirmed by several magazine profiles from the time: in a *Melody Maker* cover story published on January 18, 1997, the writer suggests that 'the romance at play in "Saturday Night" is of a subtly tragic kind. Whatever makes her happy on a Saturday night. But you can't escape the feeling it isn't making him happy, if I've read it correctly.'

'Um, no,' says Brett, 'That's one of the few songs I've ever written that is quite straight. I tried to latch onto a really common emotion: taking your girlfriend out. The intention is purely optimistic. Maybe there's a sadness and a depth to the music which colours what you hear. Maybe if it sounded like Chas & Dave.'

You can sense Brett's annoyance—Chas & Dave were a real thing back then—and Brett was only trying to tell it like it was.

'Saturday Night' has also been accused of starting off like 'Song For Guy', and of being Suede's attempt to come up with their version of 'I Say A Little Prayer'—I told you the song got a lot of flak—but in these quarters, I have to concede that my many encounters with the song have convinced me that Suede's version is just as lovely as the Whigfield song of the same name.

Perhaps, as a matter of interest—if not concern—it needs to be noted that the mix of 'Saturday Night' on *Coming Up* is one of only two that Ed Buller put his name to. The majority of the mixes on the record were completed by Dave Bascombe. Appropriately enough, Ed reveals, that, while working with him on the song in the SSR room downstairs at Mayfair Studios, Brett suddenly became very animated with the vocal he had just put down, insisting that he would only go home if they could put together a rough mix. To enable this outrageous possibility, one of these characters came up with just the right amount of coke to persuade the other one to abscond upstairs to the Neve console room.

Ed was very tired and perhaps had even been slightly bullied into mixing duties so late at night. 'I didn't like Neves,' he says now, 'but Brett was so excited—he is like a kid sometimes—and when we finally got the mix done, he went home, and him and Alan listened to it on a loop for over twenty-four hours. And this despite the fact that there was a wake next door with a body laid out and they had to be told to stop playing it.'

'Saturday Night'—like 'Lazy'—is utterly addictive, and it's hard not to see how Brett became obsessed with it for a wee while: it's dripping in reverb and clever enough to boast a Solina string machine, a cute shaker, and just about the most perfect drum pattern courtesy of Simon Gilbert. However, it's only as the song canters towards its delightful conclusion that you notice how the deceptively simple countermelody has somehow sealed the deal.

And here I would like to point out that, as any pretentious art critic will tell you, there's a difference between simple and *deceptively* simple.

'Saturday Night' became the third single off *Coming Up* to reach the UK Top 10. Released on January 13, 1997, it peaked at a sprightly no.6, then concertinaed in Finland (no.7) and Denmark (no.8) and Sweden (no.11) before eclipsing these giddy heights with the no.1 spot in Iceland.

Mat Osman lets on that the song had always been intended as the album's closer as 'the band had wanted to end the record on an optimistic note'. He also remembers Neil saying that 'Saturday Night' was 'the first Suede song you could do your hair to'. Of course, those of you who've been lucky enough to marvel at the state of Neil's hair over the years might be prompted to remark, 'That's easy for him to say.'

16

A MATTRESS ...
LIKE IN A SQUAT

> **❝**I neglected to mention how inordinately/
> inappropriately proud I'd been of the
> fact that Brett had refused to wink for
> the cover shot—the magazine always
> insisted that their cover stars winked
> to acknowledge the *i-D* logo.**❞**

'I'd always loved Peter's work, of course. I even painted my own mural of the Unknown Pleasures sleeve on my bedroom wall at home when I was a kid.'

The image used as the artwork for *Coming Up* proved to be something of a departure from the band's previous excursions into the art world. *Suede*, the band's eponymous debut album, had caused controversy with its gender-ambiguous cover image, although Brett said he chose it not just because of the ambiguity but instead 'because of the beauty of it'. The image of the androgynous, kissing couple was lifted from the 1991 book *Stolen Glances: Lesbians Take Photographs*, and, with similar propriety, *Dog Man Star* boasts a cover photograph lifted from one of Brett's old photography books, *Frontiers Of Photography*. The image used on the cover—titled *Sad Dreams On Cold Mornings*—was snapped by American photographer Joanne Leonard in 1971. When asked why he'd decided to use this particular image to adorn the album's front cover, Brett said at the time, 'I just liked the image, really, of the bloke on the bed in the room. It's quite sort of sad and sexual, I think, like the songs on the album.'

So what to do with *Coming Up*, a record like no other release in the Suede canon thus far? Naturally, Brett turned to the one person he always trusted to advise him on such matters—his mentor, of sorts: Nude label boss Saul Galpern. Saul confirms that, up to this point in the band's career, the artworks were put together on an ad hoc basis. 'Brett would go to the library,' he says. 'Or bring various books into the Nude office with images he wanted to use for the sleeves. We then had to go about finding the source of those images, and in some cases this took weeks and we kept missing deadlines, as this was pre-internet and we had to get signed agreements via fax and hard copy.' After the success of Suede's eponymous debut and the 'relative' success of *Dog Man Star*, the band were getting busier and busier, and it made sense to have 'more of a clear direction and start thinking about working in a more normalised way'.

Enter Peter Saville, an art director and graphic designer best known for his record sleeve design for Factory Records, a label he co-founded alongside Tony Wilson and Alan Erasmus in 1978. Brett tells me that it was Saul who suggested meeting up with Saville—although it was actually Nude's product manager, Yvette Lacey (later Boyd), who came up with the initial idea. Suffice to say, deadlines wouldn't prove any easier to meet.

Saville's iconic images that subsequently adorned Joy Division and New Order's finest releases were something to be admired amongst their fans—and, for that matter, anyone else who came across them—but it was Peter's artwork for *Unknown Pleasures* that had obsessed Brett as a teenager. Naturally, Peter's classic, modernist designs were immediately recognised as being an integral part of Joy Division's (and latterly New Order's) identity. It's not surprising that Brett thought Peter would be a perfect fit for a record that was always meant to be about real life as he saw it. Having said that, it was Peter's work with Roxy Music on their

Flesh + Blood album that had really caught the eye of Saul Galpern. Saul was a long-term Roxy fan, and he keenly set about arranging for Brett and Peter to meet.

'At the time, Peter had something of a reputation as a playboy,' Brett says now, 'although all the stories of his Mayfair lifestyle are hilarious and not untrue. Somehow, there was never anything seedy or naff about it, and the afternoons in the 90s spent chatting over double espressos and looking at arty photographs of scantily clad women are fond, lovely memories for me, and the *Coming Up* sleeve was something that slowly formed from those endless, spooling conversations.'

Initially, Saul remembers Peter being somewhat reluctant to become involved in designing any more record sleeves. 'He kinda suggested that he thought he was too old to understand what *the kids* wanted these days and he'd moved on from that part of his life,' says Saul, 'and as he was now working with big fashion houses and large exhibitions, it seemed like a non-starter.' But Peter loved Suede. 'Brett and I met, and I said something to him that it had never been necessary for me to say to any client before,' he revealed in Mike Christie's 2021 Sky Arts documentary on *Coming Up*. 'I am a fan.' Suede 'made music that embraced issues that you were interested in, other than just the music,' he continued, 'and in agreeing to do it, it was on the one condition, that Brett would be the executive creative director; that brashness, that brightness, the feel of that cover, of the image that we made, is entirely informed by the aesthetic and state of mind of Brett

Anderson.' Subsequently, Peter and Brett developed a special friendship. 'I'm so glad they hit it off,' says Saul now, 'because their friendship inspired and spawned those incredibly iconic sleeves of the *Coming Up* era.'

After their first encounter, Saul remembers spending several afternoons in Peter's swanky, two-thousand-square-foot Mayfair apartment—a setting that reminded him of 1970s television private-detective dramas such as *The Persuaders* or *The Saint*. Peter had only recently moved in, and he was working with Hacienda designer Ben Kelly to turn the place into a celebration of 1970s 'shag pad' styling. Naturally, Saville preferred to refer to it as his *Garçonnière*—although, funnily enough, it was officially called *The Apartment*—and Saul tells me that, 'Every time I went there, we usually had to wait a good half-hour before he appeared from the bedroom. And there was usually someone else in the bedroom that would follow him and leave through the front door. He told me that he usually dined every night at the Groucho or Le Caprice, where he wouldn't arrive until at least 10:30pm. This was confirmed when I was at the Groucho one night and he turned up just after 10:30.'

Brett's first encounters with Peter coincided with Peter's discovery of the kind of advances in image-manipulation software that enabled him to digitally rework images, rather than having to work with sourced imagery. Presumably this graphics technique would latterly become known as something called Photoshop—hey, we've all heard of it—and Peter soon began to apply the process to commercial projects like ad campaigns for the fashion designer John Galliano at Christian Dior, as well as personal projects such as his ongoing series of *Waste Paintings*. This technique was something that Peter employed to great effect on Pulp's superb *This Is Hardcore* album, released on March 30, 1998. That particular album's sleeve artwork boasted a Saville-directed cover photo shoot by John Currin—best known for his figurative paintings of exaggerated female forms—and the final, approved photograph would end up being digitally manipulated by Saville's long-term accomplice, Howard Wakefield. The subsequent media storm resulted in posters for the album on the London Underground system being defaced with graffiti stating 'This Offends Women.'

Some kind of serendipity meant that when Peter and Brett first met, Peter was already working on a project with renowned fashion photographer Nick Knight, and as Knight had just been commissioned to photograph Brett for the cover of the September '96 issue of *i-D* magazine, they were not complete strangers. I mentioned in an earlier chapter how Brett had turned up spectacularly late for that session, although I'd neglected to mention how inordinately/inappropriately proud I'd been of the fact that he had refused to wink for the cover shot—since the magazine always insisted that their cover stars winked to acknowledge the *i-D* logo—an event I celebrated by cavorting around the Savage & Best offices, whilst slapping a copy of the magazine on each member of staff's desk and announcing, 'Look, no winking: his eye is merely in shadow,' as pompously as I could get away with. It made sense, therefore, that Knight would be chosen to photograph the images for the album's sleeve, as well as the five single sleeves that accompanied the release.

The designs for all the attendant covers were put together by Howard Wakefield, and they were not entirely without incident: there were constantly missed deadlines, the cost of the artwork soon escalated into the realms of excess, and Saville himself ended up on the cover of the 'Filmstar' single artwork. 'Brett and Nick Knight ganged up on me,' Peter remembers fondly, after he'd initially been offended at the suggestion that he might possibly resemble the image of the 'faded, washed-up film star' required for such high jinks. And then there was the artwork for 'Lazy', which appears to have happened just by accident: one afternoon, whilst Brett and Saul were chasing a long-missed deadline for that single's artwork at *The Apartment*, Peter admitted that he was struggling for inspiration—until Saul picked up a piece of artwork off the floor that had somehow 'missed' the bin and said, 'What about this?'

These days, Brett says that he loves the *Coming Up* artwork as it has 'a visual language of its own, but it's still very much in Suede World—the druggy sensuality, the stark mattress'. Peter, of course, is diplomatic enough to suggest that 'covers and music become synonymous with one another', but for my part, I think Brett was just relieved that he didn't have to delve any further into his collection of 1970s photography, and he could hand the whole process over to someone as capable and talented as Saville. For the record, you should know that Brett's favourite Suede sleeve of all is *Sci-Fi Lullabies*, the double album featuring B-sides from the singles that were released from the band's first three albums— 'the stark beauty of the wrecked plane as it is reclaimed by nature somehow being such a powerful metaphor'—but *Coming Up* was the first Suede sleeve that had actually been *designed*, and Saville had still managed to make it bright, yet mysterious and enigmatic all at the same time.

As you're no doubt aware, the three young hipsters—Lee, Leah, and Paula—draped over that mattress on the cover are just the kind of people who could find themselves draped over such a thing in a cheap and nasty bedsit. The mattress was Brett's idea— 'I want a mattress . . . like in a squat' was his pronouncement at the time—as its presence implies no affectations, making do, and hints at the possibility that all three of the participants included in the image are casually involved in that most casually-accepted type of relationship: the polyamorous sexual or nonsexual liaison.

Or perhaps they just share a bedsit, and it's all a bit tight for space.

17

GOING TO CUBA FOR THE LIGHT

"By the time we arrived in Kowloon, the band were all laughed out, and it was all they could do to perform one of the most exciting gigs that that part of China had ever seen. Indeed, if the Chinese authorities would forgive me, I'd like to suggest that people were standing up and smiling, and even hugging each other."

'It's the greatest song I ever wrote, and it's got this awful video.'

I'd never previously attended a record-company meeting at a doctor's surgery in Harley Street, so, when the call came, I was ready. Indeed, the last time I'd checked, Soho, Kensington, and all corners of west London seemed to be the *environs desirable* for ruining the careers of the artists and musicians I'd stumbled across in recent years, and I was intrigued to be present at the inauguration ceremony of an entirely new set of coordinates, shyster-wise.

And, after all, the caller was quite insistent.

'Is that Savidge—of Savage & Best notoriety? Wonderful stuff! I should tell you, you're not an easy person to track down!'

Of course, this had always been the point, but I didn't let on, since anyone who knows me—and that includes you—knows that I am always striving to be as elusive as possible. Indeed, I had done some recent research on the subject of whether it was morally reprehensible for a publicist to remove themselves from a list of *available* publicists in the relevant telephone directory. It was, but I did it anyway.

'I can't believe you haven't got a mobile phone yet,' the caller continued. 'Anyway, I wanted to talk to you about an act I am working with and wondered if you are free to see me later this afternoon. I know it's short notice, but I am a doctor'—he said this as if this made a difference—'and I have a practice round the corner in Harley Street. Would you be free at 3pm this afternoon?'

I consulted my non-existent diary and agreed that I would be free.

Four hours later, I found myself sauntering down one of the more salubrious yet innocuous-looking streets with a W1 postcode and marvelling at the preponderance of middle-aged men and women of Middle Eastern appearance. Each and every one of them seemed to be sporting a gammy leg and a servant in tow. This, at the very least, is how Wimpole Street struck me at the time. On Harley Street itself, however, time and ambition seemed to have been abandoned around the year 1974. When, presumably, the local authorities had also run out of paint.

I found the address easily enough, pressed a buzzer on a door, and a voice invited me in. The inside of the building did not suggest I was at the nub of the fulcrum of the epicentre of the record business—nor did it suggest I had stumbled upon the glazing on the cherry on the icing on the cake I'd been looking for—but I must have embraced these circumstances as part of a process of disarmament I was now used to: *How many desperate, hopeful, and desperately hopeful, terminally ill souls*, I wondered, *had crossed this very same threshold, looking for salvation at the end of a surgeon's knife?* And was I any better—or worse—off than these terminally ill souls in my quest for the squillions of pounds that would allow me to escape from the hellhole that was the music industry? Indeed, haven't we all stumbled across the scruffiest and most worn-out restaurants known to humankind and found them to be worthy of Michelin Star attention?

Whilst you are pondering these words, I am noticing some other, perhaps more poignant and hastily scrawled words on a door in front of me.

GLOBAL TALENT RECORDS.

I must say that I hadn't been so excited for quite some time—not since I had come across Ocean Fresh Fish in Archway Road, N19, or Global Carpets, a decidedly un-global like enterprise situated just around the corner. Of course, it is a justified true belief that the more amateur and shambolic the affair, the more unnecessarily pompous and self-important the operation must appear to the outside world. Indeed, the enormity of the exercise almost overwhelmed me.

After the initial confusion my appearance always generated at the time, a voice from behind a desk says, 'Ah, you must be Savidge? Pleasure to meet you. I am Dr Stephens.'

The voice belongs to a handsome middle-aged man. He is dressed in an expensive-looking suit and, as he speaks, he stands up, towering over me. If prompted, I would have confessed that I had never seen anyone who looked more like a doctor in my entire life.

Dr Stephens explains that he has stumbled across a fantastic new musical duo. He is not in the habit of embarking upon ventures he has no background in, but he has decided to break with tradition and is now managing the duo, as well as financing

217

their musical endeavours. He has even founded a record label—*Global Talent Records*—in order to release their songs. The idea is that once these nascent starlings' initial recordings have proved to be a huge success, the record label will be signing and releasing albums and singles by the *crème de la crème* of British and perhaps worldwide talent.

I realise that in the light of comparatively recent developments in the nature of music-business funding, the venture we were discussing won't seem that unlikely. However, I can assure you that at the dawn of a new century, the good doctor's idea struck me as somewhat novel, and, indeed, not at all foolhardy. Of course, as the intervening twenty years have passed, I have lost count of the dads and the mums and the aunts and the uncles and the rich businessmen and women, as well as the offshore tax havens and tax-free incentive schemes, that have invested hundreds of millions of pounds into a record industry, and a profession, I was no longer glad to be part of.

I think we can both see where this is going.

Dr Stephens seemed no more or less knowledgeable than anyone else I'd ever encountered on my record-company travels, so I listened with great interest as he told me how much he was willing to spend in order to make 'the project' a success. He had made his millions, so he explained, by treating the rather personal and perhaps delicate ailments of the rich and famous, had proved himself an invaluable lifesaver on several occasions, and had been handsomely compensated for his time, expertise, and efforts in this regard. Some of his patients—I suppose we should call them clients—were even well-known pop stars, with the usual attendant tantrums and tiaras, and it was with great assurance that he suggested they would be happy to know that their untold riches were indirectly funding the artistic exploits of younger and presumably less fortunate individuals than themselves.

We *cut to the chase*—his words not mine—and talked about consultation fees and monthly retainers, finally agreeing on a strategy whereby I advised him and the band on what songs to release, and in what order, and which of these should be sent to what media, and which journalists would be most sympathetic to the band's music. Naturally, this is standard procedure for all press officers and product managers tasked with promoting and developing any ongoing music-based project from humble beginnings to 'a level of success and sustainability we can all be happy with'. By this stage, I had grown into the conversation, and these were my words and not his, but as we spoke I wondered whether I was the first person to start becoming more interested in the income than the outcome.

And then he played me some music.

Naturally, like most interested benefactors, Dr Stephens was over-enamoured with the extraordinary nature of his discovery, and he took every available opportunity to interrupt the recordings with comments on the significance of the band's lyrics, and how the duo had *stolen from the best and borrowed from the rest*. Correspondingly, he pitched them as *The Thinking Person's*

Everything But The Girl, perhaps not realising that EBTG were about as *thinking* as you could get, and that to suggest otherwise was an act of such naivety that we should all have been arrested by the Proper Rock and Pop Authorities before we'd left the premises.

The band had decided to call themselves McCabe—although I never asked why—and comprised best friends, or perhaps a boyfriend and girlfriend, or brother and sister duo with a uniquely sexually/emotionally charged relationship that only a publicist could ever hope to optimise in the grander scheme of things. Individually, they were Jenny and Matt, and from the promo shot I saw briefly, I guessed they were young enough to have a chance of making it and yet old enough to know better. By which I mean to say that they were in that netherworld twixt twenty and thirty years old.

I left the meeting clutching a cassette containing three songs, together with the realisation that I was now part of a process that had been set in motion at some point in the distant past, the details of which I would never be fully aware of. The three songs—'Nothing', 'Bungee Jumping On The Stock Exchange', and 'I Made You God'—were intended as the contents for a debut EP they hoped to release as soon as all the other elements of their campaign were in place.

At this point in proceedings, I feel it's my duty to let you know that, as much as our wannabee pop stars, McCabe, fancied themselves as something more significant than the sum of their constituent parts, a 'Male and female acoustic pop duo reach for

220

the stars!' headline might have been pushing it a little. And, if this sounds like the well-worn cynicism of a music-industry goddess, then you've hit the nail on the head.

And so began the process of advising the good doctor, on a weekly basis, as to the best course of action when it came to releasing McCabe product into the marketplace. Of course, the best course of action for him was not necessarily the best course of action for me, so this involved me suggesting that he should put the duo's single and album back by another week whenever we spoke, whilst confirming that he was willing to pay me for the privilege to do so.

To a large extent, my delaying tactics worked like a dream, although no prevarications on my part could prevent Dr Stephens' suggestion that his talented charges needed to shoot a video for the lead track on their EP as soon as possible. I mean, what was I meant to say? Videos are a waste of money? That the band weren't yet quite ready to have their musical wares captured in this way? That videos were not a useful way of promoting a band in this day and age? Whilst all of the above may be true, try explaining this to someone with deep pockets and several pop-star clients who concurred with his vision of how to hit the musical jackpot.

Naturally, I used my charm and experience to conjure up a recommendation that there were better courses of action than to shoot a video—*send them to pop school for a few years whilst still paying me* was one of my suggestions; *let the band remain mysterious by never making any videos or releasing any records at all* was yet another—but to no avail: McCabe were going to shoot a video, and that was the end of it.

One day, Dr Stephens called me into another meeting in his office.

'I know you have some mixed feelings on the subject,' he said. He looked me up and down to see if he was able to diagnose any physical symptoms associated with the mental disorder he now blamed for my irregular advice on all matters McCabe. 'But we have decided to shoot a video as soon as possible.'

My heart sank: the world would now be able to see what McCabe were all about, and my inaugural foray into *The World Of Selling Out* would be coming to an untimely end.

'The good news,' he continued with a flourish, 'is that you don't have to worry about an imminent release. We are shooting the video abroad. In fact, we are going to shoot it in Cuba, as the light is so much better over there.'

I swam in the guilt-ridden waters of this kind of idiocy for quite some time before my casual indifference was punctured by another development: McCabe had been booked to appear live in front of a selection of new university undergraduates at a venue in Battersea during freshers' week. And all attempts at suggesting that the performance should be put back by a week fell on deaf ears.

When I arrived at the venue, it was packed out to such an extent that a fire-safety official would have had a field day. Mind you, it was an odd crowd: everyone was aged around eighteen or nineteen years old, and unfeasibly drunk—so far, so good—but each member of the audience was also dressed in black. It felt like I had accidentally stumbled into some kind of goth convention. For a moment, I was transported back to my university days, when I used to dress up to see bands like Death Cult, Danse Society, and Flesh For Lulu at venues like the Garage and Rock City in Nottingham.

With considerable effort, I managed to fight my way through the massed gothic contingent in order to deliver some wise words to McCabe, who, I'd heard, were safely ensconced backstage. They seemed pleased to see me, although I could tell they were in a state of unease, presumably perpetuated by the madness they had witnessed on their journey to the dressing room. I wished them good luck and reassured them that everyone out there was so drunk they would welcome a distraction provided by live music.

Back amongst the crowd, I smelt both sick and confusion: the assembled throng had now been waiting so long that they seemed on the verge of rioting or fainting. A man dressed as a character from *The Rocky Horror Show* appeared on stage and approached the microphone. The crowd began to laugh and shout, and I got the distinct impression that the man was a well-known lark around these parts, and, quite possibly, a member of their teaching staff.

The noise emanating from the music from the DJ and the audience was deafening, but somehow the man on stage managed to call for order and the crowd became silent.

'Ladies and gentlemen, boys and girls,' he shouted with more force than was really necessary. 'Thank you for being so patient whilst the powers that be sorted out the equipment on stage. I hope you are ready for some live music. I know I am, so please put your hands together and give a big warm welcome to . . . *THE MACABRE*!'

The place went wild—for at least ninety seconds—before the shy, demure, boy-and-girl acoustic-pop duo we have all come to know and love, as a band called McCabe, shuffled on stage and assumed their rightful positions in the spotlight.

And then they started playing.

It wasn't their fault. There had been a mix-up. And no one either in the audience, or amongst those that had arranged the show, had expected a performance so inappropriate to the surroundings. There was booing and laughter, although I can assure you that only one of these reactions emanated from my direction.

It is entirely possible that our intrepid, acoustically challenged heroes managed to reach the end of their set without being lynched, but I have no way of knowing. As I dashed out of the venue, I caught sight of several members of the audience still laughing and resolved never to attend such an event ever again.

Or appear in public, for that matter.

* * *

The reason I've told you all this is because I want to talk about the subject of Suede videos, as there were five of the wretched things that turned up to accompany the five Top 10 hits that emerged from the *Coming Up* album sessions. However, before you all get too excited, I have to confess that the quote I have used as the introduction to this chapter is something of a misnomer as it refers to the video that accompanied the release of 'The Wild Ones', which, whilst being one of the greatest songs Brett ever wrote, is also one of a plethora of Suede singles that have failed to benefit from any visual interpretation/representation of their merits as pieces of music. Nevertheless, I can assure you that the quote works as a generic comment about the succession of videos that have been commissioned to illustrate the wares of all the band's singles over the years—which, if truth be told, have never lived up to the task in hand.

We used to have a standing joke in Suede World that surfaced at every Suede photo session or video shoot I attended during the 1990s. There were other standing jokes, of course—and, presumably, several I was never privy to—and I remember spending far too long with the band (for their liking) sitting on a tour bus, and then a ferry, and then another tour bus—okay, by this point it was a limousine—between Hong Kong island and Kowloon in March 1997, as the band were about to embark upon the first ever standing-up gig in mainland China. The band were now basking in their newfound success engendered by the release of *Coming Up*, although we seemed to spend the bulk of these journeys dissolved into a state of comic apoplexy, whilst contemplating the thousands of standardised black-and-white ten-by-eight promo pictures the band had been forced to sign since landing on eastern shores.

'Here's one,' said bass genius Mat Osman. 'Look, it's fucking priceless: totally uncontaminated by Suede squiggles, and consequently worth a fortune in the current market. But see here how I sign it and it becomes worthless!'

I cannot tell you how the printed page sucks the life out of such colloquial juvenilia, but a kernel of comedic truth was pursued, nonetheless.

'I have ten more unsigned photos here,' Simon Gilbert would counter, pulling a bunch of prints out of another A4-sized folder that had miraculously appeared in front of us. 'If I can just smuggle these over the border without any of us signing them, we're paper millionaires.'

I'm not saying that we all chipped in at this point, but we all chipped in at this point, and hilarity ensued. By the time we arrived in Kowloon, the band were all laughed out, and it was all they could do to perform one of the most exciting gigs that that part of China had ever seen. Indeed, if the Chinese authorities would forgive me, I'd like to suggest that people were standing up and smiling, and even hugging each other.

Back on these shores, the video shoot was proceeding unremarkably.

'How come we never get to go anywhere exotic for our video shoots?' Brett would ask, wildly gesturing at the surroundings and attendant debris one usually associates with Suede's UK promotional duties of an ocular nature.

'I mean, we always end up in a studio in Shoreditch,' he'd continue, 'but Duran Duran got to go to Rio, for fuck's sake! And

226

when they weren't in Rio, they'd be photographed or filmed on boats and beaches in the most ridiculous places.'

He had a point. Way back in 1993, Suede's debut single, 'The Drowners', spawned an albeit-excellent video—directed by one of Saul Galpern's closest friends, Linda Heymann, who'd actually thought up the name for Saul's record label, Nude—that could just as well have been shot in a chip shop, and subsequent visual escapades hardly pushed the boat out, location-wise. 'Metal Mickey', directed by Heymann again, is all butchers shops and androgynous Veruschka lookalikes wandering through tube stations, whilst the band perform in their living room; the eerily prescient, BRIT-nominated 'Animal Nitrate' video, directed by Pedro Romhanyi, features another Suede live performance, coupled with sped-up council home histrionics; 'So Young', directed by David Lewis and Andy Crabb, who went on to make the superb 'Introducing The Band' Suede tour film, is a non-performance video of sorts and may be the band's favourite as it's so honest and innocent—although perhaps this is only because the band stroke and hug their instruments whilst accompanied by various children who appear to be on fire in the countryside; and epic interim single 'Stay Together' traps the band indoors to such an extent that you can almost sense their frustration as high-rise shenanigans take place in cities all over the world, none of which appear to involve them.

Inevitably, Saul, who commissioned every Suede video from signing the band in 1991 up until their initial break-up in November 2003, believes the 'Stay Together' video to be the worst

Suede video ever made. 'It's truly awful,' he tells me, 'but it had a lot to do with the amount of substances taken by the director and the band throughout the shoot and at the editing suite. In fact, I am sure that the video contributes to the band's dislike of the song to this day.'

Saul reveals further that he'd originally contacted director Mike Leigh with a view to Leigh coming up with 'a very British, Leigh-like storyline'—what else!?—to a film encompassing the full eight-and-a-half-minute version of the song. Leigh was interested enough to arrange to meet the band at the Nude offices, but as he arrived ten minutes early and Suede hadn't arrived some forty minutes later, he decided to leave. Of course, Brett and Bernard turned up five minutes after he'd left, but it wasn't meant to be: *Welcome To Suede World*.

Oddly enough, after 'Stay Together', visual excursions took a turn for the worse when Suede shot the video for their sixth single, 'We Are The Pigs'. Directed by David and Raphael Vital-Durand, the video showcased the band appearing as large-screen inserts in an unfolding dystopian *Big Brother*-esque drama featuring burning cars, cross burnings, and several menacing-looking individuals wearing pig masks, and was initially banned by some TV stations, including MTV, for being too violent. However, the video would only serve to cement the band's top spot in a chart comprising *Bands Who Shall Never Be Captured On Camera Outside The Comfort Of Their Own Milieu*. It was an ignominious accolade, although one they immediately threw into the dustbin of history with the release of 'The Wild Ones'.

'The Wild Ones'—released on November 14, 1994—shot to no.18 in the charts, and the video, directed by Howard Greenhalgh—Saul chose Greenhalgh after seeing the latter's brilliant video for Soundgarden's 'Black Hole Sun'—cost £150,000 and was nominated for a BRIT Award for Best Video Of The Year. Brett, however, remains un-enamoured. 'That video really annoys me,' he once commented, 'because it's the greatest song Suede ever wrote, and it's got this awful video. It makes me shiver. That fucking video gives me night thoughts.' Naturally, there is a reason for this: the video was shot on a wet and windy Dartmoor with no home comforts in sight. The experience must have proved somewhat traumatic, as the band's next video, for 'New Generation'—shot by Richard Heslop—saw the whole band playing in a crowded room surrounded by broken television sets and dilapidated furniture while a group of children danced or sat around.

Back at the video shoot, Brett had bigger fish to fry—and this time, perhaps, fish of a more exotic nature.

'The next single we release is gonna have a first line which categorically states that I'm lying on a beach in Acapulco,' said Brett. 'Then they'll have to fly us out there for the video.'

For a moment, Brett appeared pleased with himself, before reality hit him hard—like a bus that the band could only ever dream of being filmed on.

'Although, come to think of it, I know what's going to happen when I speak to the director:

'Mr Anderson, we love your song and the way you have catapulted yourself into an unlikely scenario where you are lying on some sand in a beach resort on Mexico's Pacific coast. We know what you are trying to do here—and it's very funny—but, as we all know, the true essence of your humdrum existence is located within the grim, stainless-steel, pebble-dashed, nature of your songs—with a pram in the hallway and a kid on the way—and it is our moral duty to ensure the video reflects this fact. You are a genius, and we intend to capture this genius, by demonstrating to the rest of the world that you are even cleverer than they think you are! We can do this by shooting you and the band, lying on a bunch of sand—don't worry, we know people who can arrange these things—in one of our studios.

'In Shoreditch.'

As if to confirm my suspicions, Saul tells me that the reason Suede never got to film videos abroad—or anywhere sunny for that matter—was because most directors thought they wouldn't like to do something glamorous. 'Maybe they thought they were too po-faced indie; the band had the final say on treatments but, budgets aside, if they wanted to film something in, say, Brazil, they only had to say it!' Now he tells us! But you can see how we got here: the first line of 'The Drowners' is *'Won't someone give me a gun'* whilst 'Metal Mickey' kicks off with, *'Well, she's show, show, showing it off then'*. Subsequently, 'Animal Nitrate' hardly helps the overseas cause with *'Like his dad you know that he's had | Animal nitrate in mind'*, and when 'So Young' arrives with *'Because we're young | Because, we're gone'* and 'Stay Together' enforces the status quo with '*Come to my house tonight | We can be together in the nuclear sky*', what are we supposed to think? Well, perhaps not that the inaugurating lines to 'We Are The Pigs'—'*Well, the church bells are calling | Police cars on fire*'—and 'The Wild Ones'—'*There's a song playing on the radio*'—might necessitate the band renewing their passports any time soon. Indeed, by the time I heard 'New Generation' was to be the third single off *Dog Man Star*—first line: '*I wake up every day to find her back again*'—I had almost entirely given up the ghost. I did, however, have high hopes for *Coming Up*, a record that went on to spawn five Top 10 singles.

Those five singles—'Trash', 'Beautiful Ones', 'Saturday Night', 'Lazy', and 'Filmstar'—struck me as ideal fodder for *Overseas Excursions Of The Televisual Kind*. Until, that is, you heard their first lines. Indeed, '*Maybe, maybe, it's the clothes we wear*' ('Trash'), '*High on diesel and gasoline*' ('Beautiful Ones'), '*Today, she's been working*' ('Saturday Night'), '*Here they come with their make-up on*' ('Lazy'), and '*Filmstar, propping up the bar*' ('Filmstar') all suggested that Brett was in cloud cuckoo land if he thought the band would be frequenting sunnier climes in the foreseeable future.

Correspondingly, 'Trash', directed by David Mould at Elstree Studios, homes in on the whole band performing in a crowded, upmarket bar decorated in garish primary colours, whilst 'Beautiful Ones', directed by Pedro Romhanyi, features images of the band (shot in black-and-white) intercut with quick edits of conceptual segments that illustrate the song's lyrics. I could go on—and frequently do—but 'Saturday Night', starring Keeley Hawes and directed by Romhanyi again, shot on the London Underground at a disused Piccadilly Line platform at Aldwych station, reeks of claustrophobia and was perhaps a step too far; watching these videos now can only lead to the conclusion that thousands of air miles remained unclaimed.

And so it is with a heightened sense of despair that I have to tell you that Romhanyi's final shot at success—for the fourth single, 'Lazy'—was colloquialism writ large: featuring slow-motion shots of the band relaxing inside a bedsit, the video sees Brett peering through a tiny gap in the floorboards into his neighbour's apartment, almost as if to say, *Get me out of here*; and, when keyboardist Neil Codling is shown laughing whilst feeding a mushroom to some goldfish before Brett and Neil's faces combine in a mirror as one, you realise the band are never going to escape their immediate surroundings. But 'Filmstar'? A perfect opportunity to shoot the band in amongst a Hollywood backdrop was summarily dismissed in favour of a video (directed by Zowie Broach) shot in black-and-white and in a live concert setting. Events had now reached their critical mass.

Naturally, the truth of the matter is that Suede being filmed on a beach in Acapulco just doesn't work—just as Marilyn Manson relaxing in a sauna is not something that sits well with our understanding of the way something like Marilyn Manson works. Or to be blunt for a moment, don't fuck with the status quo.

Unless you actually are Status Quo.

18

HOW DID THEY DO THAT?

❝Of course, the lyric is so cleverly nuanced as to be completely innocuous in nature — it could just as easily be referring to a hot bath full of ice-cream chocolate as the more disorderly nature of some sexual practice it is asking us to contemplate.❞

'*I've always been a believer in the power of the song and that good music will carry you through. And these things go in cycles, don't they? There had been this three-year period where everyone was so interested, dissecting us and hailing us, and you can't go through that without experiencing the downside. Someone left the band and people felt they could kick us around. And I completely lost respect for the music business. I began to see it in its true colours: a gang of sheep who were too afraid to contradict popular opinion.*'

It's easy to underestimate the extent of the hyperbole that accompanied Suede's inexorable rise to the top of the UK rock'n'roll firmament during the 1990s. When I first saw them live, in 1991, I was absolutely transfixed by their sense of *otherness*, and one of their songs in particular made me check myself to see if I was really seeing and hearing what I thought I was seeing and hearing. *Isn't that what rock'n'roll is meant to do to you?* I ask myself now.

The song in question was 'Pantomime Horse' and the centrifugal line—'*Have you ever tried it that way?*'—felt charged with such effortless sexual ambiguity that I was forced to consider several enquiries:

Are they allowed to say things like this?

Are we all allowed to think like this?

Will I be arrested for thinking like this?

Of course, the lyric is so cleverly nuanced as to be completely innocuous in nature—it could just as easily be referring to a hot bath full of ice-cream chocolate as the more disorderly nature of

234

some sexual practice it is asking us to contemplate—and I had only ever come across anything as artistically enlightening as this once before: as a teenager, I had read Ian McEwan's first full-length novel, *The Cement Garden*, and been moved to distraction by the young narrator's casually dismissive view that his father's death may have been brought on by his own disinterest in his father's heart condition. The scene where the son affects exhaustion to emulate his father's genuine lack of breath—brought about by their combined efforts to deal with several bags of heavy cement they are manoeuvring around the house—opens the book, and it affected me deeply. I remember thinking, *I love my dad to bits, and yet I also love what McEwan is doing here.*

Naturally, Suede were the kind of band you could easily fall in love with, and when I found myself doing just that back in the early 1990s, it was love of the *head over heels* variety. At the time, I was trying not very hard to make a name for myself as a PR— hey, I only wanted to be loved—and by weight of circumstance, and after some overenthusiasm on my part and that of the media, the band ended up on the cover of the *Melody Maker* under the banner headline 'The best new band in Britain'. This much you know, but the accompanying article, penned by Steve Sutherland, acclaimed Suede as 'the most audacious, androgynous, mysterious, sexy, ironic, absurd, perverse, glamorous, hilarious, honest, cocky, melodramatic, mesmerising band you're ever likely to fall in love with.' At this point in the narrative, I would like to encourage all of my readers—and aspiring writers—to avoid ending any sentence with a preposition, but, in the absence of all good sense, I have to tell you that . . . I couldn't have put it better myself.

The article went on to suggest that 'Pantomime Horse' 'fair whiffs of sodomy' and that Brett sings it 'like some world-weary, habitually hysterical musical hall dame'. Subsequently, Brett goes on to defend the merits of the song with the comment, 'When you're actually involved in sex, when you're going through the motions, you're thinking, *What am I doing?* I think that's the difference between men and women—women actually enjoy sex and men enjoy thinking about it.'

The moment I read Brett's comments about 'Pantomime Horse'—and the ephemera of insight that surrounded it—I was as smitten as anyone, but I also suspected that every journalist who might subsequently stumble across the band would be of a similar disposition. *What a find*, I no doubt thought at the time, and, what's more, *the band belong to me more than they belong to any of that lot!*

Oh, the follies of youthful arrogance, I hear you cry, and no doubt didn't think at the time, but, as a publicist, I am sure you can understand that I had a different take on what was now unfolding in front of my eyes.

It is a matter of historical/hysterical record that my early teenage years almost coincided with the onset of the punk-rock movement at the tail end of the 1970s. Naturally, I am forced to use the adverb *almost*, due to the fact that there are so many conflicting opinions on the subject of exactly when the UK punk movement could ever be considered to have become *onset*: did it coincide with the Sex Pistols appearance at Manchester Free Trade Hall in April 1976—attended by the great and good of every significant punk band to have subsequently formed as a consequence—or should we acknowledge the release of the Damned's 'New Rose' single on October 22, 1976, as UK punk's *Year Zero*? As you can tell, I am pretty big on Year Zeros—although punk's Year Zero is the Year Zero to end all Year Zeros—but whatever the truth of the matter, I have little doubt that punk music was the only reason I survived my teenage years, and that *almost* is as good a way as any to describe my *Jenny-Come-Lateness* to the party.

By which I mean to say that I didn't attend that earth-shattering Sex Pistols gig in April 1976, nor did I buy that 'New Rose' single on the day of its release some six months later. Instead, my first experience of punk rock as a tangible entity was when I attended my first ever live concert on March 23, 1978. The venue for this life-changing event—at least as far as I was concerned—was the King's Hall in Derby, a building that turned out to be a recently converted swimming pool. Of course, as it was my first gig, I had no way of knowing whether all swimming pools were now being converted into venues for the benefit of the punk-rock movement, but the line-up on the night suggested that this would have been one of the more agreeable motions put forward at the most recent sitting of Derbyshire City Council's Arts, Crafts & Anarchy subcommittee, as it included The Prefects, Patrick Fitzgerald, The Slits, and the headlining band I had signed up to see, the Buzzcocks.

At this nascent juncture in my ongoing lack of sexual development, I had already discovered the aural delights of the Pistols, The Jam, The Clash, and the Stranglers, but the Buzzcocks were something else entirely: formed in Bolton in February 1976, the band actually opened for the Sex Pistols in Manchester in July later that year, a follow-up to the Free Trade Hall gig that Buzzcocks' lead participants, Pete Shelley and Howard Devoto, had helped to organise. Naturally, by the time the band had gotten around to playing my neck of the woods in 1978, Devoto had already left to form post-punk pioneers Magazine, and punk was perhaps not such a recent phenomenon; but even though my fucked-up, cut-up jeans were too tight to move in, I pogoed as if my life depended on it.

If you must know, the band that really changed my view of reality that night was The Slits: just seeing an all-girl punk outfit who didn't seem to care what anyone thought of them and what they sounded like—for the record, they looked and sounded like the most astonishingly beautiful collection of human beings I had ever looked at or listened to—made me sit up and take note. Even though I was already standing up, in case someone expected me to pogo.

Naturally, *pogo* was never going be *le mot juste* when talking about—or going to see—a band like The Slits, but how was I to know: I was only fifteen years old at the time. But then I saw Siouxsie & The Banshees at Rock City in Nottingham, and I found something else to believe in—it is a matter of public record, at least in the British Library Of Proofs And First Editions, that the first chapter in my first book was originally titled 'Why Can't I Just Be Siouxsie Sioux?'—before obsessions with R.E.M. and The Smiths and Sonic Youth and all points in between quickly followed. And then, five years later, when I saw Suede for the first time, I couldn't believe my eyes: was it possible that a team of scientists had managed to come up with the most perfect approximation of what I wanted in a rock band? And had all that fumbling around in the dark—by which I mean to say, my all-consuming habit of listening to John Peel's late-night show under the bedcovers on school nights when my parents thought I was asleep—proved to be the ideal precursor to my subsequent infatuation?

The answer to these questions is . . . *yes, probably*, but as I accompanied Suede on their tumultuous ride through several complementary—and some not so complimentary—media storms, and a career trajectory that would have frightened off most careers advisors, I couldn't help thinking, *Those who live by the sword, die by the sword.* Several more clichés spring to mind—after all, a cliché to me is like a red rag to a bull—so it was with a heavy heart and a terrifying sense of inevitability that I approached the press campaign for *Coming Up*.

I was not the only one.

On September 2, 1996, just as *Coming Up* was finally seeing the light of day, Brett's fear of being abandoned by both public and media alike must have been approaching pandemic proportions. Indeed, these days, it's with the benefit of hindsight that Brett tells me that, whilst making *Coming Up*, 'Everything was still beautifully instinctive, and I think you can hear that crackle of confidence in the record. There's a brilliant snottiness to it, a kind of *fuck you, this is us, deal with it* sort of vibe that can only feel right when it comes from a gang of young men drunk on their own self-belief.' Of course, hindsight is a wonderful thing, but Brett goes on to suggest that there was an odd paradox going on at the time—that the industry had sidelined them to such an extent that he remembers 'feeling almost a sense of exile, which further added to the bunker mentality of making the album, the us-against-the-world-ness'. Nevertheless, they were 'wonderful times, troubled, carefree, glorious and reckless, and life stretched before us, waiting to be taken'.

Ed Buller readily admits that he had been incredibly nervous about the prospect of *Coming Up* being a critical and commercial success. 'I was expecting the press to trash them,' he says now. 'Suede were Marmite at the time, and every meeting I had with record company A&R people—about other projects—I was told that they were done for. I told them that the new album was all hits and ignored them.' Funnily enough, Ed hardly witnessed the album's inexorable rise to chart success, as he upped sticks to San Francisco a few weeks after the record's release in order to fulfil production duties on another project. He stayed in San Francisco for over six months, but he vividly recalls hearing 'Trash' on the radio in the UK just prior to his departure. 'It sounded really amazing,' he says, 'and that was a special moment.'

240

Indeed, 'Trash' was as good an indicator as any that *Coming Up* was going to *make it*—a week prior to its release, music-industry bible *Music Week* had already given it 'Single Of The Week', heralding it as 'their most disciplined and direct pop nugget to date' and suggesting it 'should be their biggest hit and augers well for their September album'—but you could hear the sighs of relief as far away as Haywards Heath when the album eventually surfaced and the reviews came in. The new poppy and direct sound was hailed by the *Daily Telegraph* as 'a defiant reminder of what made Suede so special . . . if *Dog Man Star* was their *Diamond Dogs* then this is Suede's *Ziggy Stardust*, extravagant, steeped in glam and unashamedly poppy', whilst *Select* magazine called it 'a wondrous pop album, simultaneously immediate and full of scope, a lovely, charming mix of absolute beauty and the thrillingly awkward'. The *Guardian* was similarly enthusiastic, proclaiming that, despite the album's simplistic composition of 'vibrant three-minute howl-alongs, it still manages to avoid being too mainstream and incomparable to rivals Oasis and Blur'. It was only the *Independent*'s Andy Gill who remained a harsh critic. 'Two albums and one guitarist later,' he wrote, 'they sound utterly mined out; in many ways, it's a step back from *Dog Man Star*—and their manner grows increasingly obnoxious.'

Of course, we have been here before—you may remember that Gill remained unmoved by Suede's performance at the Phoenix festival, an event I enthused about when we embarked upon this journey some time ago—and, naturally, you can't please all of the people all of the time, but Gill's comments exist in stark contrast to the vast weight of critical analysis that came down on the side of the record being *something out of the ordinary*. Naturally, Suede have always been *out of the ordinary*, but it wasn't until they started to tout the album's wares in a live context that the critics could finally have their field day.

It was also around this time that I started to develop the habit of going into Suede's dressing room after every live show, just to tell them I thought they were the best band in the entire world. You can rest assured, there was no skulduggery involved— the process was not as 'creepy' as it may sound—and I believed the truth of the sentiment to the core, but I can't help thinking that my motivation was partially driven by a perceptible lack of *certainty* on Suede's part. I remember starting off with telling them they had been 'alarmingly good' at an early *Coming Up* show, and then progressing to 'outrageously good', 'indecently good', 'unfathomably good', 'ubiquitously good,' 'illegally good', and 'litigiously good', before I got to around the fifteenth show and the band were starting to seek me out and I became trapped in an ever-increasing hyperbolic hybrid, meaning I had nowhere else to go; by the end of the tour, I could be seen loitering suspiciously in the corridor outside the dressing room, and had taken to offering, wistfully, 'really rather good', when we all knew the process had outlived its usefulness.

But as we all know now, I needn't have worried: in an *NME* live review that appeared on October 12, 1996, under the banner headline 'I'll forget you Butler', James Oldham began his eulogy thus: 'And to think we thought they were finished. To think we attached so much importance to Bernard Butler. How wrong we were. Suede, for the first time in their lives, are now a proper rock band. We know they've been through stuff. We know about the instant adulation, the madness and the disintegration, the drugs and the expanding waistline and of course the alleged rebirth but perhaps we didn't believe it. We needed to see how they looked, how they carried themselves. And we never believed it would be this good. They're a gang. They've distanced themselves from the pack. They don't look like labourers who struck lucky.' And then, with a flourish, he concluded, 'They look like the Velvet Underground.'

Select was similarly approbative, semi-referencing the Velvets again: 'The image is one of not-quite-right rebellion, a pill-popping ad copywriter's notion of mid-60s New York cool.' And two months later, by the time the *NME* reviewed the band live again—at Manchester Apollo—the hyperbole was in full swing. 'Suede have finally earned that Best Band On The Face Of The Planet And Quite A Few Of The Nearer Stars Too subtitle by doing everything better than everyone else,' screamed the magazine with undue abandon, and I could have kissed its very pages—except we weren't out of the woods yet.

* * *

Suede had kicked off their *Coming Up* press campaign with a harmless-enough *Arena* article featuring Brett and writer Hanif

Kureishi quizzing each other about their lives and works, and a *Vox* magazine cover piece quite firmly in the *jury is out* drawer of press intrusions. *Vox*, if you remember, was a publication that had never presented itself as anything other than a dissenting voice against the rest of the British media's collective love for all things Suede, and the magazine's obstinately competitive streak towards rival music monthly magazine *Select* meant that it was never going to treat the band as anything other than an anomaly—a tactic that had culminated in the Brett/Bernard interview fall-out that helped initiate the band's singer/guitarist split back in 1994. But *Coming Up* felt like the dawn of a new era, so why not bury the hatchet?

Unfortunately, when the August '96 edition of *Vox* magazine appeared—'SUEDE: THE GRAND RETURN OF BRETT-POP'—in July, the first thing you noticed was how Brett seemed to have backed himself into a corner. Indeed, when he challenged 'any other band that's doing well to lose a key member and carry on and make great stuff. It requires a fuck of a lot of belief in yourself and quite a lot of talent,' I couldn't help being reminded of that magnificently petulant and adolescent couplet in 'Beautiful Ones' about babies going crazy. And then, when challenged about the rise of Blur during Suede's recently enforced absence: 'Our position at the moment is quite false because our trajectory was interrupted. I wouldn't like to be playing football stadiums if what I was playing to the assembled masses was a load of my-old-man's-a-dustman crap, pretending that you come from the fuckin' East

End, when you're a fuckin' member of the landed gentry.' Talk about aggression.

Brett went on to suggest that, unlike Blur, Suede had never been false about anything they'd ever done. 'I've never tried to come across as anything I'm not,' he said. 'I find this whole inverted snobbery thing about music incredibly condescending to the working class. I come from the background that these people are talking about. Every penny I have, I've spent the last ten years slogging for. When you come from a very poor family—which I do—you try and better yourself. It's not trying to pretend that you buy your clothes from jumble sales.' Talk about defensive.

Of course, the headline that turned all this aggression and defensiveness around arrived courtesy of *Select* magazine, and if 'How did they do *that*? Comeback of the century' wasn't going to convince the doubters, then I didn't know what was. You can imagine my excitement, therefore, when I read the accompanying article—written by Dave Cavanagh, one of the best rock critics of the last thirty years and a man who had provided the most erudite and considered critique of *Dog Man Star* in *Mojo* magazine back in 1994—and began to sense that we had crossed a line somehow and hard-nosed cynicism had been thrown to the dogs. '*Coming Up*,' said Cavanagh,' is the record that a five-piece makes when it's getting on incredibly well,' although perhaps I was more bowled over than usual by the magazine's profile of yours truly next to a similarly sized profile of Suede 'fan' David Bowie—*who knew?* etc.

As the significance of Cavanagh's superb retrospective took

shape, I noted Brett fairly cantering through a press campaign that took in far too many interviews for his liking—but just the right amount of front covers—and a philosophical approach that enabled him to tell the *NME* that the band's recent success (with *Coming Up*) was a kind of karma for all the unnecessary criticism the band had received in the last couple of years. 'There were a lot of people with their knives out who had it in for us,' he moaned, 'not because of any of the music we were making but just because we had a guitarist leaving the band. But, you know, you've got to suffer the blows, haven't you?'

Indeed, you do, but, as it turns out, it's the guitarist who replaced *that* guitarist who sums it up best. 'I'm immensely proud of *Coming Up*,' says Richard Oakes now, 'and feel that every member of Suede was firing on all cylinders when we made it. The story was almost the exact opposite by the time we started writing *Head Music* in 1998—communication in the band had broken down and everyone's personal problems had started eclipsing the music, which it never did on *Coming Up*. I don't really know why that was, maybe just success and the relaxation and excesses that inevitably follow it. It felt like the creation of *Coming Up*, the recording, campaigning, and touring of it, used up so much of our young energy, we were totally spent by the end of the tour in September '97. It would have been a bad mistake to make *Coming Up: Part 2* in 1998, but the change of direction we ended up taking was such a muddled one that we totally lost the gang feeling and collective focus that we had in '95, '96. For the next two albums I was never quite sure what to do or write, but for *Coming Up*, the goal was clear and the making of the album was so much fun, we really hit the nail on the head.'

Fun? Is that what this is all supposed to be about? I mean, at *the end of the day*—and how I envy my readers encountering such lame terminology at such a *sine qua non* stage of these legal proceedings—what are we saying here? That *Coming Up* was such an energy-sapping brute of a record that Suede had nothing left to give as the new millennium loomed beyond the horizon? Well, perhaps, but those next two albums that Richard is talking about were as good as anything Suede have ever released: *Coming Up*'s follow-up, *Head Music*, may have been afflicted by a more electronic sound, Brett's apparent crack addiction, and Neil's devastating struggle with chronic fatigue syndrome—the latter resulted in Neil having to abandon all live and promotional duties with Suede for much of the next chapter in their life story—but the album still went to no.1 in the UK, becoming the band's third and final chart topping album.

I am sure that the vast majority of my readers, whilst perhaps not having a working knowledge of how the music business operates, will understand that you're only as big as your last hit, and the massive turn around in Suede's fortunes that accompanied the release of *Coming Up* was always going to make *Head Music* a *straight out of the blocks* success. The album marked the departure of Ed Buller from production duties, and the arrival of Steve Osborne—famed for his ground-breaking production work with Happy Mondays, amongst others—meant that the band were nowhere near their comfort zone, and the new experimental direction was always going to end up with oddities like 'Crack In The Union Jack' and 'Elephant Man', as well as some of the band's most accomplished and well-loved songs to date, such as 'Electricity', 'Everything Will Flow', and 'Indian Strings'. Having said that, there was no shortage of detractors. *AllMusic* suggested the album was all 'gurgling analog synths and canned, old-school drum machines . . . essentially just window-dressing, since the songs themselves are extensions of the glam flash of *Coming Up*', and when *Uncut* magazine—ostensibly a funkier, more rounded, artistic version of the recently folded *Vox* magazine, and an offspring of the same publishing house, IPC—summed up proceedings with an eighteen-page 'special' chronicling Suede's ten-year history next to the headline 'Brett Anderson on a decade of decadence and debauchery', several hearts sank. Ironically, it was left to our old friend, the *Independent*'s Andy Gill, to kick against the pricks, hailing the record as 'broader in musical conception than their previous albums' and Osborne for bringing 'a more groove-oriented approach to the band's sound which is slicker and smoother than before, and better reflects the band's "chemical generation" outlook'. Well, you can't please all of the people all of the time.

The success of *Head Music* was relatively short-lived, and, although lead single 'Electricity' became Suede's sixth Top 5 hit in a row, the album itself slipped out of the Top 20 within three weeks of release. The band spent the next three years using seven different recording studios and four producers before Stephen Street (of Blur, Smiths notoriety) saved the day and pulled *A New Morning* out of the bag. The album cost an estimated £1 million to make but peaked disastrously at no.24 and remains the only Suede album not to be released in the USA. By the time it finally surfaced in September 2002, Neil had already been replaced by Alex Lee of Strangelove, and Brett would later tell *Filter* magazine, 'The fact that we made this album is one of the things that I regret most about Suede's career. The band would have been loved more if we had stopped making music before this. When we made it, we were very confused about what we wanted the band to be and where we wanted it to go.'

And then there were none.

On December 13, 2003, Suede performed live at London's Astoria, Brett confirming rumours of the band's imminent demise when, amidst the turmoil of a two and a half hour marathon set, he announced, 'I just want you to know. There will be another Suede record. But not yet.' Almost ten years later, after a series of 'comeback' shows—including an appearance at the Royal Albert Hall in March 2010 as part of a Teenage Cancer Trust live event that Brett described as his favourite gig and the pinnacle of his twenty-year career, and their biggest UK show to date at the O2 Arena in December that year—they released their sixth album, *Bloodsports*. The album saw the band reunited with their talisman, Ed Buller, and was easily their most critically acclaimed record since *Coming Up*.

Less than three years later but almost twenty years after the release of *Coming Up*, Suede would once again reach the giddy heights of the Top 10 when *Night Thoughts*, their seventh studio album, debuted at no.6. *The Blue Hour*—produced by Alan Moulder and Neil Codling—quickly followed in 2018, reaching giddier heights still, debuting at no.5.

It had been a long road back.

* * *

In January 1997, a full two and a half years after the release of *Dog Man Star*, the success of *Coming Up* was now not an issue, and Brett felt comfortable enough to talk about the band's future prospects. The last four months had seen the album certified platinum, after debuting at no.1 and spawning three Top 10 singles, and it was well on its way to selling over one and a half million copies. Brett finally admitted that he had just been through a huge period of being completely down. 'It very nearly didn't turn out this way,' he told a newspaper later that month. 'I was completely aware that we'd been swept away for a while. No one was interested. It was quite annoying really—we'd made two great albums, and people forgot about it. It felt quite unjust. I suppose that period did kick us up the arse.'

And now? Arse-kicking aside, when I speak to Brett for this book, he is in the midst of performing several concerts to mark the twenty-fifth anniversary of the release of *Coming Up*. He now recalls the period associated with the album as being 'a wonderful time to be in Suede. We were still young men with all the belief in ourselves that youth can bring. As you get older making records becomes harder, not only because you face the privations of time but because staying static isn't an option, so second-guessing and self-consciousness becomes part of the process.'

Some weeks later, when I am attending one of the *Coming Up* anniversary shows, I realise I am more nervous than ever, even though I have less reason to be so this time around; Suede and I are not professionally involved, I am no longer legally required to tell them their performance was *inevitably good*, nor am I, somewhat surprisingly, the newly recruited sixth member of the best band in the world. And yet, there it is, *the fear of failure, the fear of not being right, the fear of distance*.

I needn't have worried. The venue is *illegally full*—I seem to be doing it again—but the first thing I notice as the band hits the stage is that Brett looks frighteningly skinny. 'It doesn't matter how many times they grind us down,' he yells, and I realise that I lost my bet that the first words he would utter would be '*Maybe, maybe*'. And then, as soon as he sings '*Maybe, maybe*', the place goes nuts and the rest of 'Trash' is incredible, although lost amongst the frenzy of flying arms and beer, and 'Filmstar', which follows, actually is a fucking Sex Pistols song. Of course, 'Lazy' makes me think, *I really should listen to this song again, 'cos I hate it so much*, and 'By The Sea' is as heart-breaking as ever, and, now I come to think of it, the only song from *Coming Up* they performed at the Phoenix festival all those years ago, because they hadn't yet got round to writing the rest of the album. And then Brett starts strutting around like he knows he's sexy, so it must be 'She', and 'Beautiful Ones' is quite possibly a single, and, before too long, I am shouting 'VIOLENCE!' in 'Starcrazy' for no apparent reason whatsoever. And then, suddenly, the stage lights up and strange looping guitar sounds suggest I have accidentally stumbled onto the set of *Dog Man Star: The Movie*—I wrote the screenplay, if anyone wants to see it—but no, it's 'Picnic By The Motorway', and, for some apparent reason, Brett is lying down, and when 'Chemistry' kicks in no one cares whether we've all got anything in common. Finally, the set closes with 'Saturday Night' and just about the most glorious love-in, and I remember why I am here: because it makes me happy.

EPILOGUE

I began this book with a light-hearted account of a party I attended with Suede in Paris in October 1994. No doubt most of you who are reading this book are in an advanced state of denial with regard to whether you were actually alive at any stage of the 1990s, but strangely enough the incident, or series of incidents, I remember most clearly about the Saturday afternoon—after *The Party The Night Before*—includes a series of phone calls that Suede manager's, Charlie Charlton, made to the airline company he'd booked Brett's journey back to the UK with. At this point in proceedings, there was no pleasing some people—by which I mean to say that Charlie couldn't wake Brett up—and flights were cancelled on the hour, every hour, for as long as it took to get someone out of bed. Which was a very long time indeed.

I briefly talked about this carefree strategy in my first book, if only to suggest that I was not the kind of person who could ever have been a manager. *You can bet that press officers don't have to do this kind of thing*, I thought at the time, but you can also bet that I was talking about Suede and their unique approach to timekeeping. Naturally, I don't want to suggest for a moment that the individual members of Suede didn't undertake their pop-star duties in the 1990s with the utmost sincerity and seriousness, but when compared to the modern-day pop star, their behaviour (along with countless other *alternative* bands of the era) might be seen as *disingenuous*.

Suffice to say, rock'n'roll promo activities were very different back then, and turning up late or not turning up at all, to a record label meeting, was seen as a badge of honour and noncompliance with *The Man*. Moreover, turning up drunk or on drugs to such a meeting in the 90s, would have resulted in a series of knowing glances between members of the A&R fraternity, and an internal memo suggesting that the artist's contract should be renewed.

Correspondingly, in these modern times—when are they ever not modern?—circumstances now dictate that a band or artist must turn up at record company meetings clutching their iPads and proudly demonstrating a series of Venn diagrams and spreadsheets illustrating the key areas in which they are keen to expand marketing opportunities *moving forwards*. Naturally, I still believe that any keenly ambitious latter-day pop star would prefer to arrive nursing a hangover and nervously fingering the wrap of narcotics surreptitiously hidden in the side pocket of their trousers, but it's just not worth it: indeed, at the risk of coming over as some nostalgic apologist for the twentieth century, I have often wondered how the 90s would have looked if Suede had not stuck to their guns and decided to play the corporate game.

Suede Announce Record Profits, the headline would have screamed, and then, as if to make matters worse:

Suede today reported its results for the fourth quarter and full year 1995. Underlying replacement cost profit for the fourth quarter was $2.2 million compared with $2.8 million for the same period in 1994. Full year underlying replacement cost profit was $12.1 million compared with $13.4 million reported for 1994.

'Suede have now entered a new and challenging phase of low CD and compilation album prices through the near and medium term,' said lead singer Brett Anderson. 'Our focus must now be on resetting Suede, managing and rebalancing our cost base for the new reality of lower CD prices while always maintaining safe, reliable, and efficient music.'

Suede today announced 10 cents per ordinary share expected to be paid in March.

'Throughout the work to reset Suede with our new *Coming Up* album, the dividend remains the first priority within our financial framework,' Anderson confirmed today. 'Suede is now taking action to respond to the likelihood of CD prices remaining low into the medium term and to rebalance its sources and uses of cash accordingly. We are continuing our work to streamline activity and increase efficiency throughout the band's recording activities. Total

cash costs for the Suede Group have fallen since 1994 and Suede is now taking further action to deliver further efficiencies in 1996.'

Of course, if you remove the word *Suede* from the nightmarish corporate scenario outlined above and replace it with, say, *Coldplay*, it doesn't seem so ridiculous.

CAST OF CHARACTERS

Brett Anderson—Lead vocalist of Suede, solo artist, and author of *Coal Black Mornings* and *Afternoons With The Blinds Drawn*.

Craig Armstrong—BAFTA, Ivor Novello, and Grammy Award-winning Scottish musician and film composer whose credits include Baz Luhrmann's *Romeo+Juliet*, Moulin Rouge, and *The Great Gatsby*, amongst many others.

Richard Ashcroft—British solo artist and songwriter and lead singer of The Verve.

Dave Bascombe—Renowned mix engineer who made his name in the 1980s, establishing the sounds for artists such as Depeche Mode, Tears For Fears, Peter Gabriel, Human League, ABC, and Erasure.

Brad Branson—American-born photographer and pop iconographer of the 1980s and 1990s (d. December 13, 2012).

Ed Buller—English record producer, musician, and ex-keyboard player with The Psychedelic Furs. Producer of Suede's Mercury Prize-winning breakthrough debut album in 1993, as well as their no.1 album *Coming Up* and White Lies' chart-topping-album *To Lose My Life*.

Bernard Butler—British songwriter and record producer. One of Britain's most influential musicians, he was lead guitarist with Suede for their first two albums, *Suede* and *Dog Man Star*.

Charlie Charlton—Suede manager 1992–2003.

Mike Christie—acclaimed British director whose music documentary credits include *New Order: Decades, Suede: The Insatiable Ones*, and more recently, as part of Sky Art's Classic Albums series, *Suede's Coming Up*.

Neil Codling—English musician and songwriter. Keyboardist, rhythm guitarist, backing vocalist, and co-songwriter with Suede.

Saul Galpern—Nude Records label founder who discovered Suede.

Dean Garcia—English multi-instrumentalist musician and co-founder, bass player, and programmer of the rock band Curve.

Simon Gilbert—English drummer and, aside from Brett Anderson and Mat Osman, the longest-standing member of Suede.

Andy Gill—*NME, Q, Mojo,* and latterly, *Independent* newspaper journalist (d. June 9, 2019).

Toni Halliday—English musician, lead vocalist, lyricist, and co-founder of the rock band Curve.

Elton John—English singer, songwriter, pianist, and composer.

George Michael—British-Cypriot singer, songwriter, and record producer. Co-founder, along with Andrew Ridgeley, of the pop duo Wham! (d. December 25, 2016).

Mum—Mum.

Richard Oakes—English musician, songwriter and guitarist with Suede.

Mat Osman—English musician. Co-founder of, and bassist with, Suede. Author of *The Ruins* and *The Ghost Theatre*.

Jim Reid—Scottish singer/songwriter, lead singer of The Jesus & Mary Chain, and brother of William Reid.

William Reid—Scottish musician, songwriter, co-founder, and occasional singer of The Jesus & Mary Chain, and brother of Jim Reid.

Peter Saville—English art director and graphic designer who sprang to prominence after he designed record sleeves for Factory Records artists such as Joy Division, New Order, and Orchestral Manoeuvres In The Dark.

Debbie Smith—Guitarist in the rock bands Curve and Echobelly.

Gary Stout—Suede's engineer for the band's first three albums.

Taxi—not a real taxi.

ACKNOWLEDGEMENTS

With apologies to P.G. Wodehouse...

To my daughters, Scout and Piper, without whose never-failing sympathy and encouragement this book would have been finished in half the time.

With thanks to my agent Matthew Hamilton, Tom Seabrook and Nigel Osborne at Jawbone, Brett Anderson, Richard Oakes, Neil Codling, Mat Osman, Simon Gilbert, Didz Hammond, Ian Grenfell and all at Quietus Management, Saul Galpern, Ed Buller, Charlie Charlton, Mike Christie, everyone at Savage & Best—particularly John Best, Polly Birkbeck, Rachel Hendry, William Rice, Melissa Thompson and Addi Merrill—Kle Savidge, Scout Savidge, Piper Savidge, Michèle Savidge, Samantha Preston, Sophie Williams, David Barnett, and Samantha Hand.

ALSO AVAILABLE FROM JAWBONE PRESS

Riot On Sunset Strip: Rock'n'roll's Last Stand In Hollywood Domenic Priore

Million Dollar Bash: Bob Dylan, The Band, And The Basement Tapes Sid Griffin

Bowie In Berlin: A New Career In A New Town Thomas Jerome Seabrook

Hot Burritos: The True Story Of The Flying Burrito Brothers John Einarson with Chris Hillman

Million Dollar Les Paul: In Search Of The Most Valuable Guitar In The World Tony Bacon

To Live Is To Die: The Life And Death Of Metallica's Cliff Burton Joel McIver

The Impossible Dream: The Story Of Scott Walker & The Walker Brothers Anthony Reynolds

Jack Bruce Composing Himself: The Authorised Biography Harry Shapiro

Return Of The King: Elvis Presley's Great Comeback Gillian G. Gaar

Forever Changes: Arthur Lee & The Book Of Love John Einarson

Seasons They Change: The Story Of Acid And Psychedelic Folk Jeanette Leech

Crazy Train: The High Life And Tragic Death Of Randy Rhoads Joel McIver

A Wizard, A True Star: Todd Rundgren In The Studio Paul Myers

The Resurrection Of Johnny Cash: Hurt, Redemption, And American Recordings Graeme Thomson

Just Can't Get Enough: The Making Of Depeche Mode Simon Spence

Glenn Hughes: The Autobiography Glenn Hughes with Joel McIver

Entertain Us: The Rise Of Nirvana Gillian G. Gaar

Read & Burn: A Book About Wire Wilson Neate

Big Star: The Story Of Rock's Forgotten Band Rob Jovanovic

Recombo DNA: The Story Of Devo, or How The 60s Became The 80s Kevin C. Smith

Neil Sedaka, Rock'n'roll Survivor: The Inside Story Of His Incredible Comeback Rich Podolsky

Touched By Grace: My Time With Jeff Buckley Gary Lucas